THE OUPblog TENTH ANNIVERSARY BOOK

THE OUPblog TENTH ANNIVERSARY BOOK

TEN YEARS OF ACADEMIC INSIGHTS
FOR THE THINKING WORLD

Edited by Alice Northover

OXFORD
UNIVERSITY PRESS

OXFORD
UNIVERSITY PRESS

Oxford University Press is a department of the University of Oxford.
It furthers the University's objective of excellence in research,
scholarship, and education by publishing worldwide.

ISBN for 2015 edition: 978-0-19-046188-1

British Library Cataloguing in Publication Data
Data available
Library of Congress Cataloging in Publication Data
Data available

Table Of Contents

Introduction

Upon realizing that the tenth anniversary of the OUPblog was fast approaching, our OUPblog editorial board discussed many ideas about how to mark the occasion. We wished to find a way of both demonstrating and celebrating the achievement. Other blogs and websites have come and gone, with bombastic entrances and quiet exits, maintained and neglected in equal turn. Meanwhile the OUPblog has carried on.

One great advantage of working for a 500-year-old publisher is a tendency to think long-term.

Four editors, as well as a host of deputy editors on both sides of the Atlantic, have taken the helm since 2005. Over 8,000 blog posts have already been published; the count will most likely be around 8,500 by the time the anniversary rolls around on 22 July 2015. Our authors, editors, staff, and contributors have written essays, debated in question-and-answer sessions, expounded in YouTube videos, shared expertise over podcasts, tested our knowledge in quizzes, and created a host of material that belongs to more than a simple blog. We've grown from thousands of readers to hundreds of thousands.

And so we hit upon the idea of bringing the past ten years to our readers—former, current, and new—with an e-book. I invited colleagues, former blog editors, and regular contributors to select their favorite articles to illustrate the breadth and depth of our blog publishing and to share their thoughts on each. Now, having collected, compiled, and reviewed their submissions, one key theme emerges from the many reflections: they love how the blog brings complex concepts from thoughtful authors to engage with the wider world.

From the academic concerns of journal submissions and digital research, to current events in Ferguson, Missouri, and the Middle East, from the rediscovery of literature, history, and words, to a new understanding of mundane items such as teeth, this book offers a small sample of academic insights for the thinking world from the OUPblog. Everyone at Oxford University Press will work towards the promise of more such insights for the next ten years.

Alice Northover , OUPblog Editor, 2012–present
April 2015

"The fall of Rome—An author dialogue"

WITH BRYAN WARD-PERKINS AND PETER HEATHER

> "One of the most memorable pieces for me was the dialogue I facilitated between Bryan Ward-Perkins and Peter Heather. Somehow we had two books on the fall of the Roman Empire coming out the same time. Fortunately, the authors were also colleagues at Oxford (or friendly rivals if you ask the right one). The resulting two-post epic was a delightfully easy and open exchange that generated a considerable number of comments (at least for those early days) that ranged all the way to the American Civil War and the Sherman tank. Clearly, the readers loved it and I think the authors did, too."
>
> —MATT SOLLARS, OUPblog Founding Editor (2005–2006)

Today we present a dialogue between Bryan Ward-Perkins and Peter Heather. Ward-Perkins and Heather are colleagues at Oxford University and the authors of *The Fall of Rome: And the End of Civilization* and *The Fall of the Roman Empire: A New History of Rome and the Barbarians*, respectively. Both books were published this fall and offer new explanations for the fall of the Roman Empire.

Recent scholarship has argued that the Western Roman Empire did not "decline" or "fall," but was "transformed" by accommodating new barbarian populations within the Empire's political and economic structure. You both seem to op-

pose this argument and view it as a more cataclysmic affair. How would you characterise what happened in Western Europe between 376 and 476 AD?

Peter Heather: I am entirely convinced by all the evidence that shows that the late Empire was not being torn apart by irrevocable processes of decline by the fourth century. Where I do part company with some revisionist scholarship, however, is over the argument that, because some Roman institutions, ideologies, and elites survived beyond 476, the fall of the Western Empire was not a revolutionary moment in European history. The most influential statement of this, perhaps, is Walter Goffart's brilliant aphorism that the fall of the Western Empire was just "an imaginative experiment that got a little out of hand." Goffart means that changes in Roman policy towards the barbarians led to the emergence of the successor states, dependent on barbarian military power and incorporating Roman institutions, and that the process which brought this out was not a particularly violent one.

To my mind, this view of the end of the Western Empire is deeply mistaken. Surely, there were plenty of Roman elements in the successor states, but one key institution was missing: the central authority structure of the Western Roman Empire itself. This had unified much of Western Europe for 500 years, but by 500 AD, it had entirely ceased to exist.

Despite some assertions to the contrary, the central Empire did not give up land voluntarily to the immigrant groups around whom the successor states formed. Every act of immigration except the first, in 376 AD, was opposed to the best of the Empire's strength, and even that was an attempt to make the best of an impossible situation. Likewise, every subsequent attempt by the immigrants to expand their position was resisted with determination, and for very good reason. Every loss of territory to an outside group represented a loss of vital, agricultural, tax base, and therefore diminished the Empire's capacity to maintain its armies.

What emerges from all this is that the central Empire did not pass away quietly but was fought to extinction over a 70-year period of intense struggle. As the power of the imperial centre collapsed, local Romans had no choice but to make their peace with the new immigrant powers in the land, and their survival made it possible for some (but not all) of the successor states to use some Roman governmental mechanisms. But this kind of post de facto negotiation process absolutely does not mean that the Empire went peacefully. As all the recent evidence for fourth-century economic, cultural, and political vigour might lead us to suspect, the fifth-century Empire fought a long and determined, if ultimately unavailing, struggle for survival.

Bryan Ward-Perkins: Disappointingly (perhaps) I basically agree with Peter here—neither of us has much time for the theory that the Empire was quietly "transformed," by the peaceful "accommodation" into it of some Germanic barbarians. We both believe in invasions that were violent and unpleasant, rather than what I have termed the "tea party at the Roman vicarage" theory of settlement by invitation. I probably share Peter's views because I have heard him lecture on the subject many times, always with great conviction! Anyway, the idea that the fifth century was more peaceful than violent just doesn't fit the facts. Some degree of accommodation between invaders and invaded was possible, particularly over time. But I argue that the horrors of invasion are undeniable, and were often protracted, and that adjusting to rule under Germanic masters was painful and difficult for the Romans, used as they were to lording it over the known world.

Why was the Western Empire unable to fight off the fifth-century military challenge?

Peter Heather: The old view was essentially that internal decline had destroyed its capacity to resist: moral decadence, depopulation, lead poisoning, the debilitating effects of its recent conversion to Christianity, or another internal cause of your choice. It is important to remember that the Empire had always had important limitations. The inherent limits of its largely agricultural economy meant that output could not be increased dramatically should new revenues and manpower be required to face new threats (the Romans failed, in other words, to invent either the tractor or chemical fertilisers). It had bureaucratic limits which affected its capacity to mobilise resources, and, perhaps above all, political limits. Its sheer size, especially after the rise of Persia to superpower status from the third century (see below), meant that power needed to be shared for administrative reasons, but political stability was immensely difficult to achieve. Any period of unity was always likely to be succeeded by another period of internal rivalry or even civil war. But all of this had always been true, and won't explain the catastrophic collapse of the Empire in the fifth century. In my view, the roots of collapse have to be sought in the outside world, among the barbarians. I should say that I use "barbarian" here only in the sense of "outsider" (one of its Roman connotations).

First, in the third century, a new dynasty, the Sassanians, united what is now largely Iran and Iraq with the overt aim of overthrowing Roman hegemony in the Near East. Rome, for the first time, faced a rival superpower, which quickly inflicted three huge defeats on the Empire's existing military establishment. Newer and bigger armies needed to be raised, therefore, as well as the funds to pay for them, and one Emperor was now required more or less permanently on the Persian front. The result was the so-called Third Century Crisis, which saw the Roman Empire go through 50 years of painful adjustment until, by *c.* 300 AD, this new Persian threat was parried. Parried, though, not defeated, and this is a key point. After 300 AD, Persia remained a superpower, and about a third of the Empire's forces had always to be stationed on the eastern front. This directly affected its capacity to deal with further crises elsewhere, as did the fact that most of the available fiscal slack in its generally rigid agricultural economy had already been used up to fund the larger military establishment raised to face down the Persians.

This further "barbarian" crisis duly unfolded towards the end of the fourth century on the Empire's European frontiers, brought on by the intersection of two separate phenomena. First, the Germanic world had been through a social, political, and economic revolution since the first century. Germanic socio-political units were now larger and more powerful than they ever had been before. Second, the Huns—the latest of what were clearly, in the ancient through to the later medieval period, periodic intrusions into central Europe of originally steppe nomadic groups – convulsed this hinterland in the generation after 375, especially in two particular moments of crisis, 376–80 and 405–08. By 410, enough barbarians were inside the Western Empire to push it into a vicious circle of decline as its military assets were burned up in battle and its agricultural tax base eroded by warfare and forced grants of territory made to different barbarian groups.

Once inside the Empire, the barbarian immigrant groups continued to unify, producing still larger and yet more powerful entities that the Empire could not hope to dismantle. The result was a reversal of the strategic power advantage that had brought the Empire into being, so that these new, and more powerful, barbarian groups were able to carve out kingdoms for themselves from the Empire's living body politic. This was no peaceful process, even if, in its aftermath, some local Roman elites came to terms with the new powers in the land, and hence made it possible for these kingdoms to show some Roman features.

The existence of odd Roman elements must not, however, mislead us into thinking that we are looking at anything other than a revolution. The new states that emerged were not mini-Roman Empires. Key institutional differences—the absence of professional armies funded by large-scale taxation amongst others—as well as entirely different cultural patterns in areas such as elite literacy—the Classics—mark them out as entirely different kinds of entities from the Empire which preceded them. This was a highly violent process which both marked the culmination of long-term patterns of development in the periphery of the Empire and set European history off on a new course.

Bryan Ward-Perkins: When it comes to explaining the fall of the Western Roman Empire, we both believe that a series of unfortunate events was central to the story. Events (such as the arrival of the Huns) and chance play bigger parts in both our accounts, than deep structural weaknesses. I even argue that the eastern Roman Empire, which survived until Constantinople fell to the Turks in 1453, was saved, not because it was structurally stronger than the Western Empire, but mainly because it happened to have been dealt a favourable geographical hand.

A thin band of sea separated and protected the heartlands of eastern prosperity (in Asia Minor and the Near East) from the barbarian-infested Balkans.

It is interesting that both of us should prioritize events and chance over structural change, because this seems to be the way that historians are moving right across the spectrum of historical thought. When I was a student, in the early seventies, we were all into profound structural changes, that swept people along inexorably; and we viewed events as banal and superficial. Nowadays (and probably it is just another fashion), individuals and concatenations of events, all of which might have gone differently, are seen as central to human history. In theory at least, according to modern thinking, I might be writing this sentence, not in England, but in a still-extant province of Britannia—if a few things had only gone better in the fifth century.

Peter Heather: Here, there's maybe a bit of difference between us because I do believe in the importance of structural change outside the Empire. It's the argument I start to develop in the last chapter of my book, but much more elsewhere, namely that having to co-exist with a large and aggressive Empire pushes neighbouring populations into processes of socio-economic and political change, the end result of which is to generate societies more capable of parrying the Empire that started everything off. There is, in other words, a kind of Newton's Third Law: to every Empire there is an opposite and equal reaction which undermines the preponderance of power in one locality on which the original Empire was based. This, in my view, is what happens in spades in the Near East with the Sassanians, and is already happening in important ways in non-Roman Europe, when the Huns come along to generate a precocious unity among the

Germani. But, given enough time, the Germani might have got there anyway!

How important was the fall of the Western Roman Empire, in terms of its consequences for the history of Europe?

Bryan Ward-Perkins: Peter is primarily a historian of the state and of the army, while my background and intellectual roots are mainly in Archaeology; so our approaches to this question inevitably do differ. Peter prioritizes the collapse of a great power, in terms of its political and social consequences—above all, how landed aristocrats, once operating within a finely tuned and empire-wide system of patronage and status, had to adjust to life under heavily militarized and locally based Germanic kings.

My book, and this is its major novelty, concentrates on the impact of the fall of the West on daily life, as revealed by a mass of new archaeological research over the last few decades (which I hope is presented in a readable and approachable manner). I argue what is currently an unfashionable view (though, in my opinion, it is blindingly obvious)—that the Roman world brought remarkable levels of sophistication and comfort, and spread them widely in society (and not just to a tiny elite); and that the fall of Rome saw the dismantling of this complexity, and a return to what can reasonably be termed 'prehistoric' levels of material comfort. Furthermore, I believe that this change was not just at the level of pots and pans, important though these are, but also affected sophisticated skills like reading and writing. Pompeii, with its ubiquitous inscriptions, painted signs, and graffiti, was a city that revolved around writing—after the fall of the Empire, the same cannot be said for any settlement in the West for many centuries to come.

I recommend caution in praising "civilizations" (whether Roman, or our own), and I do emphasize that "civilizations" have their downsides. But, equally, I think the current fashion for treating all cultures as essentially the same—and all dramatic changes (like the end of the Roman world) as mere "transformations" from one system, to another equally valid one—is not only wrong, but also dangerous. It evens out the dramatic ups and downs of human history into a smooth trajectory. This risks blinding us to the fact that things have often gone terribly wrong in the past, and to the near certainty that, in time, our own "civilization," and the comforts we enjoy from it, will also collapse.

Peter Heather: I never know, really, how to judge good and bad in global terms when looking at any societies. I am very sure, though, that the effects of Rome's fall were huge and felt right across the board. It's quite common now, for instance, while describing the history of subjects as diverse as Christianity or literacy in this period, to view Rome's fall as incidental or unimportant. In my view, that is straightforwardly wrong. Late Antique Christianity evolved a series of authority structures, both centrally and locally, which were shaped around and based upon the existence of the Roman state. When that went, these authority structures, even when they survived, changed their nature fundamentally. In shorthand, the medieval monarchical Papacy is inconceivable had powerful Western emperors survived. So too literacy. Patterns of elite literacy, for instance, were based upon the career structures generated by the Empire's bureaucracy—lots of jobs for those knowing a particular kind of Latin well—and once that bureaucracy went, so did the jobs and the patterns of education and literacy attached to them.

Why two books on the 'Fall of Rome' now?

Bryan Ward-Perkins: Even curiouser, both books are by scholars from the same university who know each other well. A number of potential explanations spring to mind. Firstly, that the authors hadn't communicated with each other and were rather cross to learn that the other had just finished a book on the same subject. Secondly, that it was part of a dark plot to overwhelm opposing views, and to ensure decent review coverage—since journals prefer discussing pairs of books to singletons. Thirdly, that this is a really important subject—the fall of a very great power that dominated the Mediterranean and most of Europe for over five hundred years—that hasn't been examined in detail for some time, and which cried out for two books, each with a different slant. Peter's book is an immaculately researched (and highly readable) blow-by-blow account of the events that brought the Western Empire down; while mine contains only a brief look at the causes of the fall of the West, and spends most of its pages investigating the consequences of this fall (hence my subtitle "And the End of Civilization").

Peter Heather: We both knew we were doing them, I think, but there was a huge amount of chance involved in when our research leaves fell, and hence when we were able to write them. And, as Bryan says, they are to our eyes very different and complementary books (although it would be interesting to find out if readers thought so too). In broader terms, we are certainly both responding to huge wave of interest in the late Roman period, which has unfolded since the early to mid-1970s. I myself am certainly part of this wave, but, so far, it has tended to carry scholarship forward in lots of different areas at once (mine was barbarians) and hence the energy has generated the raw material for new overviews rather than the new overviews themselves. Bryan and I are both, I think, in part pulling these many different findings together in ways that make sense to us. I would myself expect other people to start wanting to generate new, broader takes on the subject as well.

BRYAN WARD-PERKINS is the author of *The Fall of Rome: And the End of Civilization* and teaches at Trinity College, University of Oxford. PETER HEATHER is the author of *The Fall of the Roman Empire: A New History of Rome and the Barbarians* and teaches at Worcester College, University of Oxford.

Originally published in two parts on 22 and 29 December 2005 at http://blog.oup.com/2005/12/the_fall_of_rom2/ ; http://blog.oup.com/2005/12/the_fall_of_rom/

"Lincoln's finest hour"

BY JAMES M. MCPHERSON

"To say it was hard to pick one favorite post is an understatement. Even five years after leaving OUP, I remain honored and amazed by all the incredible authors who contributed to the blog during my tenure. One post that stands out in my mind as an irrefutable favorite is James McPherson's essay, 'Lincoln's finest hour.' McPherson's post is a strong reminder that politicians once valued the American people more than they valued campaigning for their jobs."

—**REBECCA (FORD) BERNSTEIN,** OUPblog Editor (2006–2010)

On 23 August 1864, President Abraham Lincoln wrote the following memorandum and asked his Cabinet members to sign it on the back side of the paper without reading it (to forestall leaks): "This morning, as for some days past, it seems exceedingly probable that this Administration will not be re-elected. Then it will be my duty to so co-operate with the President elect, as to save the Union between the election and inauguration; as he will have secured his election on such ground that he cannot possibly save it afterwards."

How had things come to such a pass? How was it possible that Lincoln, whom historians rate as America's greatest president and who led the nation to victory in its largest war, could anticipate that he would not be reelected? Precisely because, at the time he wrote these words, victory in that war appeared unlikely. The military campaigns launched by Generals Ulysses S. Grant and William T. Sherman with high hopes for imminent victory in the spring of 1864 had bogged down in stalemate and apparent failure by August after three months of the worst carnage in the war. Weary of the slaughter and longing for peace, Northern voters regarded Lincoln's leadership as a failure and were ripe for a new policy and new leadership. A week after Lincoln penned his despairing memorandum, the National Democratic Convention nominated the popular General George B. McClellan for president on a platform that declared: "After four years of failure to restore the Union by the experiment of war, we demand that immediate efforts be made for a cessation of hostilities, with a view to an ultimate convention of the states, or other peaceable means, to the end that, at the earliest practicable moment, peace may be restored on the basis of the Federal Union."

Any overture by the North for peace negotiations in such circumstances would have ensured that "the earliest practicable moment" to restore the Union would not come for many years, if ever. During the previous six weeks, two contacts between unofficial envoys of the Union and Confederate governments to explore the possibility of peace negotiations had only elicited the nonnegotiable conditions of Presidents Lincoln and Jefferson Davis. Lincoln's conditions were reunion and the abolition of slavery; Davis's condition was Confederate independence. But in the atmosphere of Northern war weariness during that dark summer, Democrats and even some antislavery Republicans accused Lincoln of a "blunder" for his insistence on abolition as well as Union as a precondition for negotiations. "Tens of thousands of white men must bite the dust to allay the negro mania of the President," declared one opposition newspaper. For that purpose "our soil is drenched in blood . . . the widows wail and the children hunger." Henry J. Raymond, editor of the *New York Times* and also chairman of the Republican National Committee managing Lincoln's reelection campaign, told the president in August that his chances for reelection were nil. "Two special causes are assigned for this great reaction in public sentiment," said Raymond, "the want of military success, and the impression that we can have peace with Union if we would but that you are fighting not for Union but for the abolition of slavery."

Lincoln came under enormous pressure to drop emancipation as a precondition for negotiations. But in what must be seen in retrospect as his finest hour, he refused to do so. He told weak-kneed Republicans that "no human power can subdue this rebellion without using the Emancipation lever as I have done." He noted that more than 100,000 black soldiers and sailors, most of them former slaves, were at that moment fighting for the Union. "If they stake their lives for us," said Lincoln, "they must be prompted by the strongest motive," the promise of freedom. "And the promise being made, must be kept. . . . Why should they give their lives for us, with full notice of our purpose to betray them? . . . I should be damned in time & in eternity for so doing. The world shall know that I will keep my faith to friends & enemies, come what will."

Lincoln's refusal to sacrifice racial justice for political advantage seemed to doom his chances for reelection. In effect, he was saying that he would rather be right than be president. In the end, however, he turned out to be both right and president. Sherman's capture of Atlanta on 2 September and other Union military victories during the fall turned Northern sentiment around by 180 degrees. The end of the war now appeared imminent, not through peace negotiations that would have virtually conceded Confederate victory but by a smashing Union military triumph. Lincoln was decisively reelected in November, and Union arms secured the unconditional surrender of Confederate armies the following spring. Several of the essays in *This Mighty Scourge* explore Lincoln's leadership as commander in chief and the strategies of Union military commanders who eventually forged that victory.

JAMES M. MCPHERSON is an American Civil War historian, and is the George Henry Davis '86 Professor Emeritus of United States History at Princeton University. He is the author of many works of history, including *Battle Cry of Freedom*, which won the 1989 Pulitzer Prize.

Originally published on 8 February 2007 at http://blog.oup.com/2007/02/lincolns_finest/

"A mystery-y-ish-y word trend: The -y suffix has gone bananas"

BY MARK PETERS

"Though I generally prefer to write humorously, this post feels like the closest I've come in the blog to writing something that could be in a linguistics journal. Recording the existence of unlikely, preposterous words such as *secret identity-y* and *mystery-y-ish-y* feels like I made a nice contribution to the literature on slang morphology. I was psyched to build on the great stuff Michael Adams has done and document some seriously whacked-out words."

—MARK PETERS, OUPblog contributor

Many lessons can be gleaned from watching reruns of *Buffy the Vampire Slayer*: Indirect sunlight is not an unlife-ender for vampires. Some small-town mayors may yearn to become giant unholy snake things (no surprise there). As Cordelia Chase said, "People, you've got to leave your tombs *earthed*." (Whoops, that was on the Buffy spinoff *Angel*—but whatever.)

Amidst these practical tips for living, a lexical lesson emerged on the Joss Whedon show: the *–y* suffix is on a rampage, and it can attach to almost anything, as shown by on-show coinages such as *crayon-breaky*, *heart-of-darkness-y*, *out-of-the-loopy*, *stammery*, *twelve-steppy*, and *unminiony*, which were discussed by Michael Adams in *Slayer Slang: A Buffy the Vampire Slayer Lexicon*. Adams follows up on the adventures of the *–y* suffix in his new book, *Slang: The People's Poetry*, which records other wild examples from the web and elsewhere, including *beliefy*, *four-lettery*, *Jesusy*, *super-protecty*, and *co-y*—a blend of prefix and suffix without a traditional root, meaning *codependent-y*.

As friends and countrymen know, I am a modest soul who wouldn't dare compete with the remarkable Adams in the octagon or elsewhere, but I'll stack my pile of wacky *–y* suffixed words up against his any day. While collecting nonce words for my dictionary-blog *Wordlustitude*, I've scooped up plenty of Buffy-esque adjectives, such as *come-hither-y*, *creepy-uncle-y*, *forbidden-love-y*, *gone-to-the-darksidey*, *homicidal maniac-y*, *pins-and-needles-y*, *post-traumatic stress syndromey*, *princess of darkness-y*, *self-hatey*, and *special-forces-y*. Nuff said on the *–y* suffix, right?

Nuh-uh. Holy guacamole, there is a *lot* more to the story.

I've noticed a sub-species of unlikely *–y* suffixed words that is even more of a wonder, words that might be the biological equivalent of discovering a wombat that is half meerkat and maybe one-eighth Don Rickles: words like *military-y*, *Monday-y*, *prophecy-y*, and *yay-y* have a double-y construction that shows the *–y* suffix is even more versatile than Adams imagined and the Buffy writers demonstrated.

Before getting to the good stuff, it should be noted that odd-looking *–y* suffixed words are not entirely new-ish and Buffy-influenced. The *OED* records some infrequently used older terms with a contemporary zing: *weekendy* (1930), *newspapery* (1864), *skeletony* (1852), *gossamery* (1790), and *heatheny* (1580) are just a few examples. One oldie in particular is the lost cousin of the words I've been collecting: *clayey*, which popped up as far back as 1024 and is still turning up more recently: "PS: Don't text during ceramics class, gets your phone all clay-y" (17 March 2009, Off-Screen I Ramble).

In an e-mail interview, Adams said "As you know, when it comes to word formation, almost anything is possible, but when a word ends with a vowel, it's unlikely to take -y." That said, Adams' own work has turned up vowel-vowel combos such as *wicca-y* and *zebraey*, while I've spotted the recently useful *swine-flu-y*. Some of the double-y words I've found are basically in the same category: *birthday-y*, *doomsday-y*, *holiday-y*, *hoyay-y*, *killjoy-y*, *Monday-y*, *slay-y*, *soy-y*, and *yay-y* repeat a letter but not a sound, so they look a little stranger than they are. That said, they are still damn strange.

Far odder and more unlikely are the double-y words where the same sound is repeated, such as *biology-y*, *Buffy-y*, *comedy-y*, *conspiracy-y*, *democracy-y*, *gravy-y*, *history-y*, *jealousy-y*, *lady-y*, *memory-y*, *military-y*, *mythology-y*, *prophecy-y*, *secret-identity-y*, *spy-y*, *strawberry-y*, *synergy-y*, *technology-y*, and *theory-y*. The repeated sound is also found in words like *bee-y*, *me-y*, *pee-y*, *squee-y*, and *tree-y*, which look more normal alphabet-wise, but are just as weird soundwise. As Adams says, "That is simply the least likely pattern, and one wonders if such forms ever occur in speech; it's a pattern easily constructed in Webtext—it's readable, even if it's not sayable."

But it is sayable! Or at least it's performable, as I discovered while watching the ultra-disturbing Christopher Reeve episode of *South Park* ("Krazy Kripples," 26 March 2003), which contained this line from a reporter: "Tom, the irony is even more irony-y as it appears that the stem cells have given Christopher Reeve almost superhuman strength." That example is also interesting for breaking the "all X-y" formula that encompasses just about all of my examples, which refer to people "being all guy-y," getting "all Hillary-y," "feeling all holiday-y," and "smelling all strawberry-y." It appears that this productive formula is stronger than the phonetic taboo of the double-y, allowing for a wide array of square, rhombus, and hippo-shaped pegs to be placed in this round hole.

But the –y suffix is also mighty, and there are other examples that show double-y words can occur outside this formula, like this *Battlestar Galactica*–related comment from *Television Without Pity*: "As for the moniker, at last night's LA show the question came up again, and we got a pretty firm response from Verheiden that it was purely an aesthetic decision, made at the last minute—they thought 'Zeus' sounded 'too mythology-y' and preferred the rhythm of 'Jupiter.'" Then there's *hoyay-y*—a variation of the fan abbreviation meaning "Homoeroticism, yay!": "I really like the Poconos one, but isn't that a bit too hoyay-y for the friendship thread?" So the formula certainly helps, but it isn't necessary to produce these whacked-out words.

Now if all that isn't enough to give you new respect/loathing for the *–y* suffix as it expands/desecrates the English language, let me make your mind go kaboom once more.

After years of weird-word collecting, I'm pretty unfazed by words with multiple, redundant, exuberant suffixes. As the collector of *battle-tastic-tacular-gasm-worthy* and *mega-legal-robo-proctologist*, it's going to take some pretty fancy suffixation to turn my head. However, even I was gobsmacked out of my chair when I spotted *mystery-y-ish-y*.

Yowza. That is a triply redundant suffix, plus a double-y, with sort of a triple-y. *Mystery-y-ish-y* is a lexical wonder, but it does have some slightly less wondrous near-relatives: I spotted *analogue-y-ish-y*, *emo-y-ish-y*, and *orange-y-ish-y* in the wild, so that particular combo of suffixes isn't a total anomaly. But it is, dare I say, in my best Mr. Spock voice, quite anomaly-y.

More evidence of extreme suffixation can be found in the following list of examples, which may inspire your own uses of the *–y* suffix. After studying the evidence, I can strongly recommend that this suffix be used with no caution whatsoever. Like doughnuts—according to Homer Simpson and my own privately funded research—it really can do anything.

birthday-y

"yay other! Hope today's all birthday-y and fun!"

(**6 Nov. 2007**, *Stationzero*)

candy-y

"decorations were amazing, i mean it's all candy-y and fantasy like . . . like from Charlie and the Chocolate Factory, they had candy trees, ginger bread house, candy house . . . and loads of HUGE christmas trees . . ."

(**25 Dec. 2006**, *The One in Penang*)

conspiracy-y

"i'm trying not to sound all conspiracy-y here (trilateralists? bilderbergers? shadow government established by the 1947 roswell alien visit?), but . . . he's not a stupid guy. i firmly believe he's advancing his agenda, whatever it might be . . .and the fact that we conservatives, his alleged base, don't like it means nothing to him at all."

(**8 Jan. 2007**, *Riehl World View*)

history-y

"But, unfortunately, the Declaration isn't official policy of any country anywhere or at any time. It was a statement of intent written by a small group of people who acted without sanction of any governing body. The US didn't exist for more than a decade after that. I mean, since we're being all history-y here."

(4 **Sept. 2008**, *The Edge of the American West*)

holiday-y

"Are you feeling all holiday-y now? All the special Chrisma-hanau-kwanza-kah feeling that's in the air, and also on Starbucks's annoying playlist is already starting to grate on my nerves."

(3 **Dec., 2008**, *Food in Mouth*)

jealousy-y

"maaan, i need to see this movie. and i'm gonna be all jealousy-y when claira gets it for Christmas. hahaa"

(**6 Dec. 2008**, Livejournal)

killjoy-y

"After fueling all kinds of fun 'What if X bought Moto?' mashups with rumors they were fleeing the handset business like a burning building, Motorola gets all killjoy-y today, affirming that they're 'fully committed' to the mobile biz. Hey, there have been bigger turnarounds."

(**11 Feb. 2008**, Matt Buchanan, *Gizmodo*)

lady-y

"My parents are awesome. My Dad's all nature-y and work-y and my Mum's all lady-y and they're both daft and then I am a super combo of their awesome points (and then their tempers >__>;;) and then yesssss. I win."

(**28 Mar. 2009**, *Ultimate Guitar Community*)

memory-y

"And now I'm all memory-y thinking about ice-skating at the rink right around the corner from that theater when I was growing up."

(**13 Nov. 2006**, *Whedonesque*)

mystery-y-ish-y

"My faith tells me that marital sex, like all acts blessed with holiness, is a great mystery — and from thence comes its beauty.

"Well, it WOULD be wouldn't it? Since Dawn's not married, she can't be having marital sex. It's all mystery-y-ish-y. And she can imagine it's pretty, if she wants."

(**23 May 2006**, *Pandagon*)

philosophy-y

"I'm sorry to get all philosophy-y here, but I think these supposedly philosophical questions matter an awful lot to the politics at stake here."

(**24 May 2008**, *Pandagon*)

secret identity-y

"And don't be all sneaky when you come in. Y'know . . . all secret identity-y, and then come back on here and post about how dumb I am and stuff. 'Cause that would be just plain mean."

(**15 Dec. 2006**, *Comic Books Resources Forums*)

secret society-y

"I love it when they get all secret society-y"

(**19 Apr. 2003**, Livejournal)

soy-y

"i've just made my latest incredible discovery—boysenberry soy yoghurt, or as i like to call it, 'soyghurt.' it doesn't upset my lactose-unfriendly stomach and doesn't taste all soy-y and is creamy and filled with delicious boysenberries and 99% fat free! and it was on special at coles barkly square! brilliant!"

(**17 Jan. 2006**, *from the irish meaning 'ditch/canal builder'*)

spy-y

"It was all spy-y and computery. The poor man's Tom Clancy, I guess."

(**16 May 2007**, *The Sheila Variation*)

technology-y

"They are orange! They are cute! They are all technology-y and stuff! They feel like nothing I've ever worn before, and they feel *goooood*!! I'm very psyched. They even come with a DVD to teach me how to wear them, they are so advanced!"

(**24 Feb. 2007**, *Asparagus and Mayonnaise*)

MARK PETERS is the genius behind the blog *Wordlustitude* in addition to being a contributing editor for *Verbatim: The Language Quarterly*, a language columnist for *Good*, and the author of *Yada, Yada, Doh!: 111 TV Words That Made the Leap from the Screen to Society*.

Originally published on 21 May 2009 at http://blog.oup.com/2009/05/y-suffix-bananas/

"John Lennon and Jesus, 4 March 1966"

BY GORDON R. THOMPSON

"Blogging can generate informative reader feedback, especially when some of the readers prove to have played a role in the narrative. Such was the case with "John Lennon and Jesus," not to suggest that either the Beatle or the religious figure necessarily had access, nor that they contacted me. However, the relevant managing editor of *Datebook* did take umbrage after my suggestion that the reprinting and the repackaging of Maureen Cleve's 1966 interview had partially motivated Lennon's assassin. Of course, causal explanations often prove to be undependable, but humans do live in and react to a symbolic world with its multivariate interpretations, and one deranged individual did come to believe that a Beatle had put himself above Christianity. One consequence of the modern globalization of telecommunications and transportation has been an ongoing debate about society and religion. Revisiting how a casual comment by John Lennon about history developed into a confrontation between cultures offers a brief glimpse into the origins of the world we now inhabit."

—**GORDON R. THOMPSON,** OUPblog contributor and author of *Please Please Me*

Forty-five years ago, in the spring of 1966, as swinging London and its colorful denizens attracted the attention of *Time*, the publishers of *Datebook*, an American teen magazine, found part of a recent interview with John Lennon to be of particular interest. A rapid disintegration ensued of the complex identity that the Beatles' management, the media, the fans, and even the musicians themselves had constructed, setting in motion a number of dark forces.

After a short promotional tour in late 1965 (about which the British media complained they lacked access to the fab four), the Beatles took time to refresh and to re-imagine their repertoire. Lennon, for his part, retreated to the lethargy of his home in suburban Weybridge, Surrey, until journalist and friend Maureen Cleave interrupted his reverie. Cleave interviewed each of the Beatles for a series of profiles in London's *The Evening Standard*, and the loquacious Lennon ruminated extensively on a variety of topics ranging from "lunch" to religion. For most of the conversation, the Beatle laments his increasingly meaningless possessions (e.g., a gorilla suit), even as he exhibits them, and predicts that he would not live much longer in his neighborhood of stockbrokers, business executives, and private estates. Musically, he reveled in Indian music, playing a disk for the interviewer until he disappointedly realized that she had little interest in or tolerance of the art: "You're not listening, are you? It's amazing this—so cool."

He moved on from that topic, ruminating about books he had been reading. In the profile, Cleave describes Lennon's well-stocked library, his interest in history (notably Queen Boadicea and the Celts), and, in particular, the history of religion. His reading about the variety of humankind's beliefs in the sacred led him to an understanding of how ideas had come and gone over time. Notably, he sensed that Christianity, like other religions, had contributed good ideas, but that something else would eventually replace it too. To that end, Lennon asserted,

"Christianity will go . . . It will vanish and shrink." As his proof, he added that currently the Beatles were "more popular than Jesus." Moreover, in reflection, he noted that even rock 'n' roll would disappear.

His comments hardly surprised his friends. In the wake of the Second World War, their generation had openly questioned the received wisdom of the existence of a supreme deity, even as they sometimes embraced exotic alternatives. Attendance at British churches had dropped precipitously in the postwar years and, by the sixties, these institutions fought a losing ideological battle with sports events and the cinema. For the Beatles, their student conversations in Liverpool and debates with their existentialist college friends in Hamburg had shaped a humanist worldview. Teenage fans in North America, particularly in the southern United States, commonly held a rather more innocent and insular view of religion.

Marketers and the Beatles management had long played on audience naiveté, and the Beatles had been part of the game. From the very beginning of his relationship with the band, manager Brian Epstein had sought to shape their image through clothing and media appearances. The films *A Hard Day's Night* and *Help!* had portrayed the Beatles as madcap comedians romping in a world where flirting substituted for sex and only aberrant religion posed problems. And if these film depictions of the band eschewed depth, the Beatles cartoon series that had debuted on 25 September 1965 confirmed these one-dimensional depictions. Thus, with the band a blank slate, every fan could project his or her own interpretation of who the Beatles were and could fantasize about the band playing at their high-school dance or visiting birthday parties. Anything was possible.

Almost from the beginning of Beatlemania, politicians had tapped the Beatles' polysemic image for their own benefit, parading the band through towns and displaying them on balconies. Religious leaders were similarly not above referencing the fab four in an attempt to attract parishioners. The Beatles themselves were aware and complicit in the farce, protecting their private lives and restraining themselves in press conferences. Better to act the fool than to tell an interviewer what you really thought. Cleave let some of that mask slip to reveal a thoughtful Lennon who questioned the value of his privileged existence and the divinity of Jesus.

When the teen magazine *Datebook* published excerpts of the interview later that summer on the eve of the Beatles' US tour, it displayed the line "I don't know what will go first—rock 'n' roll or Christianity" as one of several quotes on the cover and as the title of the article inside. Soon, two radio stations in America's south saw the marketing possibilities of the statement and banned Beatles recordings before moving on to displays that offered theatrical possibilities. Initially, the tempest that swirled around Lennon's comments had the intended effect of focusing attention on the self-righteous conservatives who burnt Beatles records in scenes reminiscent of Nazi Germany's book fires. More seriously, members of the Ku Klux Klan picketed performances and threatened violence, sending manager Brian Epstein into a frenzy and the Beatles into disbelief. Lennon gave the impression of a deer in the headlights at a Chicago press conference on 11 August as he tried to satisfy a press corps that smelled blood, saying, "I still don't know quite what I've done."

Years later, the worst would come to pass when a deranged gunman assassinated Lennon, in part over how *Datebook* had sensationalized the musician's comments about religion. As in other recent examples, those who sought to benefit by twisting shallow interpretations of reality to stir hatred in minds of the gullible probably felt little culpability.

GORDON THOMPSON is Professor of Music at Skidmore College. His book, *Please Please Me: Sixties British Pop, Inside Out*, offers an insider's view of the British pop-music recording industry.

Originally published on 4 March 2011 at http://blog.oup.com/2011/03/lennon/

"The teal before the pink: Ovarian Cancer Awareness Month"

BY GAYLE SULIK

"We would be hard-pressed to find anyone living in America who was not familiar with Susan G. Komen for the Cure, much less the flood of pink ribbons that descend upon us across the web, on our doorsteps, and in stores each October. Yet, for the millions of donors and race participates that Komen has amassed, few seem to know much about what the organization actually does, or where exactly the money goes. I've chosen to highlight the work of Gayle Sulik because she has been instrumental in bringing to light the controversies surrounding Komen and how the commercialization of breast cancer has actually helped companies profit from the disease. Her work sends the necessary message that cause marketing is not philanthropy, and not every so-called charitable organization is particularly charitable. She has challenged us to rethink the marketing campaigns that tug at our heart strings, and moreover, whether we as individuals are actually supporting the causes we have been led to believe are important."

—**LAUREN APPELWICK,** OUPblog Editor (2010–2011)

September is National Ovarian Cancer Awareness Month. Will the White House be lighted in teal just as it's been lighted in pink to commemorate National Breast Cancer Awareness Month? Will grocery stores line shelves with teal ribbon products? Will schools give out teal T-shirts or pins? Probably not. Pink has been the color of choice when it comes to cause support. Even as the sister of breast cancer (i.e., in 5 to 10% of cases, both breast and ovarian cancer have a connection to mutations on the known breast cancer genes, *BRCA1* and *BRCA2*), ovarian cancer garners relatively little public support or attention.

Some people don't even know that disease-specific ribbons besides pink exist. Nan Hart wrote on the discussion board of the Ovarian Cancer National Alliance (19 Sept.) that after her daughter got a teal ribbon tattoo on her wrist, one of her daughter's coworkers asked why her breast cancer ribbon wasn't pink? Umm . . . because it's not a breast cancer ribbon? The assumption that one ribbon, the pink ribbon, the mother of all ribbons, is the baseline of social support for cancer is indeed a huge assumption. In the coworker's defense it just shows how well pink marketing has worked to create the association. Awareness messages aside, millions of people buy, display, consume, and think pink.

An article in *Marie Claire* on the "Big Business of Breast Cancer" points out that "some $6 billion a year is committed to breast cancer research and awareness campaigns," making it a "gold mine for pink profiteers and old-fashioned hucksters." Kudos to Lea Goldman for pointing this out. Yet, for those who are working to provide information, support, and resources for other types of cancer, this story isn't "news" at all. One woman commented on the Ovarian Cancer National Alliance discussion board that she went into a Bed Bath & Beyond this month and the first thing she saw was a breast cancer "awareness" display of pink products. "Where the education or awareness was," she said, "I don't know, but they're certainly making a lot of money." Another commenter contacted various media outlets to encourage reporting about ovarian cancer during its September awareness month. Apparently they "seemed uninterested." Pink publicity, on the other hand, is now a year-round activity, and the related products? Many of them are around all year too.

Concern about the extreme focus on the pink cause to the exclusion of almost everything else is not new. Last October the blog *But, Doctor I Hate Pink* published a guest post from Sarah Sadtler Feather, who was diagnosed with ovarian cancer in 2006 and is known in the blogging community as The Carcinista. In her essay, "Pinktober from a Teal Point of View," Ms. Feather wrote:

> "Before September is even over, stores are filled with pink merchandise. Magazines fill editorial pages, poignant survivor stories and photo spreads with breast cancer awareness. We're swept off the surface of the earth by the waves of pink . . . Aside from pinkwashing consumer products and Walks For Whomever being pretty lousy ways to drum up funds for research; aside from the ubiquitous ribbons fooling people into thinking they're doing some good in the "War on Cancer" that's been failing miserably for forty years; aside from it distracting attention from preventing cancer by forcing corporations and governments to clean up toxic chemicals and environmental hazards, Pinktober overlooks the fact that there are other, deadlier forms of cancer in the world that could use some of the Pink Juggernaut's P.R. clout and donation dollars."

I wish The Carcinista were here today to comment on Pinktober 2011. She died this spring after five years of treatment for ovarian cancer.

Is the heightened attention to breast cancer just a matter of numbers?

The total number of people living with cancer (i.e., cancer prevalence) was estimated in 2007 to be 6.4 million. Of these, 2.6 million were living with a breast cancer diagnosis and 177,000 were living with a diagnosis of ovarian cancer. That's a lot of people walking around with breast cancer. However, cancer prevalence is affected by both the incidence of a cancer and how long people normally live with the disease. Those with ovarian cancer tend not to live as long after diagnosis compared to those with breast cancer. The National Cancer Institute reports that although the incidence rate for ovarian cancer has declined since the mid-1980s, it remains the fifth leading cause of cancer-related death among women in the United States. The Centers for Disease Control reported that in 2007, 20,749 women were diagnosed with ovarian cancer, and 14,621 women died from the disease. It's hard to get the word out and advocate for the cause when so many are dying from the disease. The same could be said of those with metastatic breast cancer.

With so many people being diagnosed with breast cancer, stage zero and invasive types included, the advocacy and consumer bases for breast cancer are huge. Compared to the more than 1,500 non-profit organizations dedicated to breast cancer, there are about 150 in support of ovarian cancer. That's easily ten times the advocacy/education/visibility of those working on ovarian cancer, and in the breast cancer arena the mega charities hold the greatest power of all. Pink events in cities across America from pub crawls to races call attention to breast cancer, demand media attention, raise funds, engage political leaders, shape research, and saturate the culture. The plethora of pink products spreads the message of pink importance even further. How could smaller constituencies stand a chance?

When it comes to research, Dr. Elise Kohn states, "There is no question that ovarian cancer is underfunded and underrepresented in the scientific and medical communities." The National Cancer Institute's investment in ovarian cancer research increased to $110.1 million in FY 2009, up from $97.7 million in FY 2005. The institute also supported $16.2 million in ovarian cancer research in FY 2009 using funding from the American Recovery and Reinvestment Act. (In comparison, the National Institutes of Health spends more than $700 million per year on breast cancer research, and the Department of Defense Breast Cancer Research Program has allocated about $2.5 billion to peer-reviewed research since 1992.) Despite this situation Dr. Kohn states further that "there has been an exponential and explosive growth in knowledge and treatment benefits for ovarian cancer over the last decade." Yet, the difference in research agendas and allocations and within and across different types of cancer may also reflect differences in levels of advocacy, publicity, and political will.

I'm not in support of the so-called "disease Olympics," as Chief Medical Officer of the American Cancer Society, Dr. Otis Brawley, refers to them—"when advocates for one disease try to increase funding for their disease by decreasing funding for another disease." Good science has the potential to make an impact across diseases, as Brawley suggests in "Funding the Best Science:"

> "Basic scientific research, some of it not focused on a particular cancer site, has given us so much insight into cancer that we can actually see a day in the very near future in which it doesn't even matter where the cancer started. In other words, the clinician is not going to be interested in whether it's lung cancer

> or breast cancer or colon cancer. The significant questions for treatment will be: Which genes are mutated? Which genes are turned on? Which genes are turned off? Which genes are amplified?"

This sounds reasonable to me, and I hear the same sentiment from cancer researchers frequently. A clear example would be drugs for those with breast or ovarian cancer who have mutations on the *BRCA1* or *BRCA2* genes that inhibit an enzyme called PARP (i.e., Poly (ADP-ribose) polymerase). Inhibiting this enzyme seems to disrupt chemotherapy resistance in cancer cells. Win-win, if it works. Unfortunately, the overwhelming festivity and consumption that surrounds the pink cause has created a situation in which the torch for the disease Olympics has already been lit. In the race for one cause, pink consistently gets the gold medal. Everyone else struggles not just for a place on the podium, but to be heard all.

GAYLE A. SULIK, PH.D., is a medical sociologist and was a 2008 Fellow of the National Endowment for the Humanities for her research on breast cancer culture. She is author *of Pink Ribbon Blues: How Breast Cancer Culture Undermines Women's Health.*

Originally published on 27 September 2011 at http://pinkribbonblues.org/2011/09/the-teal-before-the-pink-ovarian-cancer-awareness/ ; it was then published on 30 September 2011 at http://blog.oup.com/2011/09/teal/

"Nobody wants to be called a bigot"

BY ANATOLY LIBERMAN

"Writing a post every week for so many years, summer or winter, rain or shine, requires a lot of work, but, as I now know, the effort is worth the trouble. People respond from all over the world, ask questions, disagree, point out mistakes (catching a blogger's errors is everybody's favorite occupation), and occasionally praise. In etymology, good solutions published in fugitive journals and rarely read reviews often get lost: the truth has been unearthed but remains hidden and unappreciated. Dictionaries keep saying that *bigot* is a word of unknown origin, but I encountered an old explanation that seemed excellent to me and was happy to advertise the discovery. Also, while working on the history of *bigot*, I realized that *beggar* and *bugger* belong to the same "nest" and later wrote about both. And last but not least, the post has been noticed. Nowadays, to be noticed even for a brief moment is no mean feat."

—**ANATOLY LIBERMAN,** OUPblog columnist and author of *Word Origins and How We Know Them*

Nobody wants to be called a bigot, but accusations of bigotry are hurled at political opponents with great regularity, because (obviously) everyone who disagrees with us is a bigot, and it is to the popularity of this ignominious word that I ascribe the frequency with which I am asked about its origin. Rather long ago I wrote about *bigot* in the "gleanings," but answers in the "gleanings" tend to be lost, while a separate essay will pop up in the Internet every time someone will ask: "Where did *bigot* come from?" Wherever it came from, the word has changed its meaning since the old days. It used to mean "hypocrite; someone who professes his religious views with excessive zeal." Today a bigot is a fanatic, a dyed-in-the-wool adherent of some political doctrine (which, as pointed out, does not coincide with ours).

The questions asked in connection with *bigot* are four: (1) Does *bigot* have anything to do with the word *god*? (2) Is *bigot* (from an etymological point of view) the same word as Spanish *bigote* "moustache"? (3) Is Romance *big-* "goat" the root of *bigot*? and (4) Did *bigot*, if it was coined as a term of abuse, target some religious group? Before I answer those questions, I should warn our readers against the information one can occasionally find on the Internet and in printed sources. For example, in October 1997, the *Catholic Digest* published on pp. 117-120 an article titled "Asphalt, Bigot, and Comma." It informed the subscribers that *asphalt* goes back to Leopold von Asphalt (1802–1880); that *bigot* derives from Nathaniel Bigot (1575–1660), an English Puritan preacher; and that *comma* traces back to Domenico da Comma (1264–1316), an Italian Dominican scholar whose signature punctuation mark led to a charge of heresy by the Inquisition (commas, apparently, were not found in the earliest manuscripts of the Bible and were therefore considered an insult to God). Many other gentlemen, including Mr. Botch, Mr. Doldrum, and Mr. Fiasco, enlivened the pages of that publication. I wrote a politely indignant letter to the editor but received no answer. Beware of amateur etymologists.

According to an oft-repeated story, preserved in an old chronicle, Rollo of Normandy, on receiving the dukedom from Charles the Simple, refused to kiss the king's foot and said (in

English!): "Nese bi god," that is, "No, by god." Allegedly, this is how *bigod*, later *bigot*, became an opprobrious moniker of the duke and then of the Normans. That Rollo should have offended the king and said something in English to him is beyond belief, but it is not improbable that some such taunting name of the Normans (who had the reputation for bad manners and swearing) existed. Yet the constant association in the past between the word *bigot* and religious hypocrisy (that is, obstinate devotion to a creed) does not augur well for the *bigod* theory. Also, the story has too strong a taste of a folk etymological guess invented in retrospect to explain an obscure word. To this day French *bigot* means "excessively pious; superstitious." A convincing etymology of *bigot* should probably be sought in a religious sphere, where it had a concrete addressee; the slur as we know it must have been secondary. For comparison, I may cite *bugger*, ultimately from Medieval Latin *Bulgarus*, "heretic," because the Bulgarians belonged to the Greek Church. From Latin it made its way into French (where it already meant "sodomite"), from French into Middle Dutch, and finally, in the sixteenth century, into English.

One of the twentieth-century hypotheses on the origin of *bigot* connects it with Yiddish *begotisch*, "pious, God-loving." Only in Yiddish do we find a positive sense of a *bigot*-word. But there its structure is transparent: "(being) by God," while whether *bigot* is *bi-got* or *big-ot*, or something else constitutes the main problem. Otto von Best, the author of the Yiddish hypothesis, attempted to connect *bigot* not only with God but also with moustache, for Spanish *hombre de bigotes*, literally "a man with a moustache," means "a steadfast man, a man of strong character." Von Best reconstructed a situation in which anti-Semites heaped abuse on the Jews for clinging to their religion and refusing to shave off beards. By contrast, the Jews reviled the beard-shaving apostates. Thus did in von Best's opinion *begotisch* lose the positive connotations (preserved in Yiddish) and acquire its present-day meaning. The entire situation strikes me as rather improbable, and it remains unclear why and where the Romance languages borrowed the word *bigot* from Yiddish, but the point that in dealing with *bigot* we sometimes encounter positive or at least neutral senses is well taken, not so much on account of Yiddish as in light of Italian *sbigottire*, "to dismay" (compare *sbigottirsi*, "to be dismayed *or* amazed, dumbfounded"); *amazement* is not synonymous with *fanaticism*. (The Italian examples are from von Best's article.)

It is not my purpose to go over the rather numerous etymologies of *bigot*, for, if, as I think, the word originated as a religious slur, moustache and goats (though goats have beards) should probably be left out of the picture, which means that Spanish *bigote* has an etymology of its own. (Even if mustachioed foreigners were mocked somewhere in Europe, the taunt could not have produced the sense "an over-devout person.") By a coincidence (?), *bigot*, like *bugger*, also surfaced in English texts in the sixteenth century, though it was known in southern France 400 years earlier; it was applied to some people living there. The ingenious derivation of *bigot* from *Visigothi*, that is, Visigoths, who were converted to Christianity in the fourth century and embraced Arianism (and were, consequently, looked upon as heretics), shatters at the difference between the initial consonants and the fact that a memory of the Goths and their beliefs would hardly have lingered for so many centuries.

Several religious orders had names sounding like *bigot*: *Beghardi* (from which we possibly have *beggar*), *Beguines* (like *Beghardi*, derived from the founder's name), and especially *Be-*

guttæ. All of them, as Wedgwood wrote, "professed a religious life, and wore a distinctive dress, without shutting themselves or binding themselves by permanent vows. We don't gather from the quotations that there was originally anything offensive in the names themselves. . . . But the pretension to superior strictness of life easily falls under the suspicion of insincerity, and thus these names soon began to imply a charge of exaggeration and even hypocrisy." Note the accent on the deterioration of meaning in the course of time. Wedgwood traced *bigot* to *Begutta* (of which *Beguttæ* is the plural), but *bigot* was known earlier that *Begutta*, whatever the origin of that word is.

Of all the conjectures on the etymology of *bigot* I find the one by the French linguist Maurice Grammont (1866–1946) the best. He was so prominent as an instrumental phonetician and a general linguist, and his suggestions on early bilingual education made him so famous among specialists, that his ideas outside those two areas have been overlooked. The curse of etymological work, to the extent that it goes beyond recycling the *OED* and Skeat, is that even the most dedicated researchers cannot keep track of hundreds of notes in fugitive journals, short reviews, and chance footnotes. They miss important ideas and tend to reinvent the same creaky wheel. Grammont commented on *bigot* in a review of Bloch's French etymological dictionary (I discovered it after my bibliography of English etymology was published, so the reference is not there). As follows from the subsequent editions of Bloch's dictionary, it made no impression on its author or on anybody else. Grammont proposed that *bigot* is a shortening of *Albigot*. Albegensian heresy flourished at the end of the twelfth and the beginning of the thirteenth century in southern France, that is, exactly where and when the word *bigot* seems to have turned up for the first time. We still have to understand the semantic history of the Italian words, cited above (were the Italian Catholics bewildered and frightened, rather than disgusted, by such views?), but it may be that we do have the answer to the riddle that has seemed insoluble for such a long time. If Romance etymologists read this blog, perhaps they will respond.

ANATOLY LIBERMAN is the author of *Word Origins and How We Know Them* as well as *An Analytic Dictionary of English Etymology: An Introduction*. His column on word origins, "The Oxford Etymologist," appears on the OUPblog each Wednesday.

Originally published on 26 October 2011 at http://blog.oup.com/2011/10/bigot-2/

"Our Antonia"

BY EDWARD A. ZELINSKY

"Writing regularly for the OUPblog has been an excellent experience for me, a monthly opportunity to address pending issues of law and public policy in an increasingly important forum. However, the post I enjoyed writing most was my book review of the novel *My Antonia* by Willa Cather. *My Antonia* is a story of family, personal identity, and first love set in my home state of Nebraska. The chance to reflect on these themes makes this my favorite effort."

—**EDWARD A. ZELINSKY,** OUPblog columnist and author of *The Origins of the Ownership Society*

The first time I read *My Antonia*, I hated it. That was to be expected: It was required reading in my sophomore English course at Omaha Central High. This was during the Sixties. In the Age of Aquarius, no one was supposed to like assigned reading. That's why it had to be assigned.

I next confronted *My Antonia* in college. Like Jim Burden, Willa Cather's narrator, I had left Nebraska to go to east to continue my education. During those years, some feminists were arguing for Cather's place in the women's canon. Thus, Antonia, the Nebraska icon, was to be transformed into Antonia, the feminist icon.

This didn't seem quite right to me. As I reread *My Antonia* in college half a continent away from Nebraska, Cather's portrayal of Nebraska seemed more appealing than it had when I had grown up there. And Antonia was too rich a character to serve anyone's political agenda.

It was when my 11-year-old daughter discovered *My Antonia* that I came full circle. Jacoba was blessed with a wonderful English teacher who guided her to read challenging novels. *My Antonia* became Jacoba's favorite book. This prompted me to confront Cather's most famous Nebraska novel once again.

This time, I was really hooked as I read of Antonia, her family's travails, and her ultimate triumph on the plains of Nebraska. This book, I declared, was good; it deserved to be taken off the required reading list.

The following year, when we visited my mother in Omaha, Jacoba asked if we could go to Red Cloud, Willa Cather's hometown, which she fictionalized in *My Antonia* as Black Hawk. I told my mother we were going to Red Cloud because Jacoba wanted to. That was partially true.

Our day in Red Cloud remains one of the best memories of raising my daughter. The citizens of Red Cloud are understandably proud as they guide visitors through the many Cather-related structures still standing.

At the end of the day, our guide gently walked us toward the cemetery where Antonia is buried. The small, picturesque graveyard was dotted with Nebraska sunflowers. Standing at Antonia's grave was one of the genuinely peaceful moments of my life.

As I stood by Antonia's grave, I realized that, like Jim Burden, I had gone east to be educated and live my life as a lawyer, but that I had forever left behind an important part of me in Nebraska.

A few years later, when Jacoba's twin brothers reached bar mitzvah age, the synagogue in Connecticut was decorated with Nebraska sunflowers.

EDWARD A. ZELINSKY is the Morris and Annie Trachman Professor of Law at the Benjamin N. Cardozo School of Law of Yeshiva University. He is the author of *The Origins of the Ownership Society: How the Defined Contribution Paradigm Changed America*. His monthly column appears on the OUPblog.

Originally published on 19 December 2011 at http://blog.oup.com/2011/12/my-antonia/

"Mars, grubby hands, and international law"

BY GÉRARDINE GOH ESCOLAR

"Wrapping up my first year as blog editor, there was a great deal of excitement around the red planet. After the phenomenal landing of Mars Curiosity in August, the initial results were eagerly anticipated. As the staff searched for people to comment, we were surprised to find an international law angle to our astronomical concerns. I couldn't be more pleased when Gérardine Goh Escolar delivered a blog post combining such specialist knowledge with a sense of humor: the perfect combination for academic blogging."

—**ALICE NORTHOVER,** OUPblog Editor (2012–present)

The relentless heat of the Sun waned quickly as it slipped below the horizon. All around, ochre, crimson, and scarlet rock glowed, the brief burning embers of a dying day. Clouds of red dust rose from the unseen depths of the dry canyon — Mars? I wish! We were hiking in the Grand Canyon, on vacation in that part of our world so like its red sister. It was 5 August 2012. And what was a space lawyer to do while on vacation in the Grand Canyon that day? Why, attend the Grand Canyon NASA Curiosity event, of course!

Wait, what? *Space lawyers?* Have they got their grubby hands on *Mars* now?

Well, quite the contrary, and in a manner of speaking, space law has been working to keep any grubby hands off Mars. In the heady aftermath of the Soviet launch of Sputnik-1 in 1957, nations flocked to the United Nations to discuss—and rapidly agree upon—the basic principles relating to outer space. Just a decade later, the 1967 Outer Space Treaty was concluded, declaring outer space a global commons, and establishing that the "exploration and use of outer space shall be carried on for the benefit and in the interests of all mankind." Today, more than half of the world's nations are Parties to the Outer Space Treaty, and its principles have achieved that hallowed status of international law—custom—meaning that they are binding on all States, Party or not.

More specifically, the 1967 Outer Space Treaty affirmed that outer space, including the Moon, planets, and other natural objects in outer space (such as Mars!), were not subject to appropriation, forbidding States from claiming any property rights over them. Enterprising companies and individuals have sought to exploit what they saw as a loophole in the Treaty, laying claim to extraterrestrial land on the Moon, Mars, and beyond, and selling acres of this extraterrestrial property for a pretty penny. One company claims to have sold over 300 million acres of the Moon to more than 5 million people in 176 countries since 1980. The price of one Moon acre from this company starts at US$29.99 (not including a deep 10% discount for the holiday season)—potentially making the owner of said company a very rich man. Other companies have also started a differentiated pricing model: "The Moon on a Budget"—only US$18.95 per acre if you wouldn't mind a view of the Sea of Vapours—vs. the "premiere lunar location" of the Sea of Tranquillity for US$37.50 per acre. The package includes a "beautifully engraved parchment deed, a satellite photograph of the property and an information sheet detailing the geography of your region of the moon." Land on

Mars comes at a premium: starting at US$26.97 per acre, or a "VIP" deal of US$151.38 for 10 Mars acres.

Indeed, the US$18.95 may be a good price for the paper that the "beautifully engraved parchment deed" is printed on. And that is likely all you will get for your money. Although the Treaty does not also explicitly forbid individuals or corporate entities from laying claim to extraterrestrial property, it does make States internationally responsible for space activities carried out by their nationals. Despite these companies' belief that the Treaty only prohibits *States* from appropriating extraterrestrial property, it is disingenuous to say that on Mars and any other natural object in outer space, "apart from the laws of the HEAD CHEESE, currently no law exists." International law does apply to the use and exploration of outer space and natural extraterrestrial bodies, including Mars. And that international law, including the prohibition on the appropriation of extraterrestrial property, applies equally to individuals and corporate entities through the vehicle of State responsibility in international law, and through domestic enforcement procedures.

Now, that's not to say that the principle of nonappropriation is popular. It has been questioned by a caucus of concerned publicists, worried that it would stifle commercial interest in the exploration of Mars. Some other publicists—myself included—have come up with proposals for "fair trade/eco"-type uses of outer space that they contend should be an exception to the blanket ban. But the law at the moment stands as it is—Mars cannot be owned. Or bought. Or sold. For many private ventures into outer space, that is a "big legal buzzkill." These days, it seems, NASA may even land a spacecraft on the asteroid you purport to own and refuse to pay parking charges—and the US federal court will actually dismiss your case as without legal merit. What is the world coming to?

On the bright side, international space law has meant that there has been a lot of international cooperation in outer space. This has mostly kept the peace in outer space (no Star Wars!) and has ensured the freedom of the exploration and use of outer space for the benefit of humanity. International space law has also contributed toward keeping the Martian (and outer space) environment pristine. And in a world where we worry about the future of our own blue planet, maybe having international law keep our grubby hands of her sister Red Planet isn't such a bad idea after all.

DR. GÉRARDINE GOH ESCOLAR is Associate Legal Officer at the United Nations. She is also Associate Research Fellow at the International Institute of Air and Space Law at Leiden University, and has taught international law and space law at various universities, including the National University of Singapore, the University of Cologne, and the University of Bonn. She was formerly legal officer and project manager at a national space agency, as well as counsel for a satellite-geoinformation data company. She is the author of *International Law and Outer Space*. All opinions and any errors in this post are entirely her own.

Originally published on 10 December 2012 at: http://blog.oup.com/2012/12/mars-grubby-hands-and-international-law/

"The dire offences of Alexander Pope"

BY PAT ROGERS

"Pat Rogers's post on Alexander Pope is entertaining, informative, and instructive in equal measure. Pope isn't a popular poet in the manner of William Wordsworth, yet he's responsible for some of the most famous phrases in the English language. In a short space Rogers tells us why *The Rape of the Lock* is such a brilliant poem, how Pope creates his effects, why he is such an important and influential poet and satirist, and how his targets have so many parallels in the modern world. Above all, Rogers's enthusiasm, his combination of broad description with close reading, his erudition and ease of communication encapsulate the essence of Oxford World's Classics—and he makes you want to read Pope!"

—JUDITH LUNA, Senior Commissioning Editor for Oxford World's Classics, Oxford University Press

---

There's never been a shortage of readers to love and admire Alexander Pope. But if you think you don't, or wouldn't, like his poetry, you're in good company there too. Ever since his own day, detractors have stuck their oar in, some blasting the work and some determined to write off the writer. A noted poet and anthologist, James Reeves, wrote an entire book in 1976 to assail Pope's achievement and influence. But it has never succeeded; Pope, a combative as well as a marvellously skilled author, keeps coming back for more. He produced more first-rate poems than anyone else in the eighteenth century, as we might guess from his fame across Europe and his huge appeal in America before and after the Revolution.

In truth, much of the hostility he faced in his lifetime had to do with fear of his scathing wit. "Yes, I am proud; I must be proud to see / Men not afraid of God, afraid of me," he wrote late in his career. The stark clarity with which he states the idea must have made quite a few contemporaries shuffle another step backwards.

It doesn't take much more to enjoy Pope than a reasonably good ear and a feeling for language. To read his works carefully will give anyone a grounding in how lines sing, how to make words bend and let meanings fold into each other. It will spare you a whole module on the creative writing course. Sound and sense are delicately adjusted, rhyme and rhythm subtly integrated, wit and wisdom dispersed with the utmost economy.

The most single brilliant item is *The Rape of the Lock*, completed in 1714 when he was only 25. On the surface this relates how a brutal upper-class twit attacks an airhead socialite. You can find the tale amusingly retold by Sophie Gee in her novel *The Scandal of the Season* (2007). Actually the ravishing of a beauty in this ravishingly beautiful poem amounts to cutting off just one of her curls, but the text constantly insists that a more serious violation has gone on.

What Pope does is imbue this episode with layers of submerged meaning. Though it is easy to follow the narrative, the events are just the excuse for a dazzling exercise in channelling literary sources, which makes the allusive structure of *Finnegans Wake* seem almost a doddle. *The Rape* supplies a ridiculously miniaturized version of classical epics like *The Iliad*, with heroic battles fought at a card-table; an appropriation of *Paradise*

Lost; a reinvention of the fairy lore in *A Midsummer Night's Dream*; a subversion of fanciful occult systems such as that of the Rosicrucians; a satire on court life under Queen Anne; and a dramatization of the limited marriage market for the gentry among Pope's own Catholic community. It plays with arcane connections associated with the seasons and the times of day; makes fun of fashionable pseudo-medical ideas linking hysteria to women's biology; and cruelly exposes the consumerism of a materially obsessed society, while rendering the texture and glitter of its luxury objects in enticing detail.

The main trick is to build up this critique from a phrase, a verse, a couplet, a paragraph, and a canto, all serving as fractals which contain within themselves the central paradox announced in the first two lines: "What dire offence from am'rous causes springs, / What mighty contests rise from trivial things." The contrasting terms here form what we call "antithesis," borrowing an expression originally used in classical rhetoric. Pope extends antithesis to his grammar, his versification, his metaphors, and his narrative.

A single bit of wordplay encapsulates this process. It comes in the famous pun that describes the queen's routine at Hampton Court, where she "sometimes counsel take[s]—and sometimes tea." In the previous couplet, British statesmen plot the fall of "foreign tyrants," but also of "nymphs at home." Everything from the tiniest unit up to the overall shape of the work is designed to enforce the same balanced oppositions between the grand and the slight. And none of it ever ceases to be funny.

Pope's supreme technique meant he could excel in almost every genre available to him. His powerful satire *The Dunciad* makes mincemeat of the vapid scribblers in Grub Street. You don't have to know who they were to get most of the jokes. *An*

Epistle to a Lady might have been written as a set text for modern feminists, so provocatively does it raise issues on the gender front for debate and appraisal. *An Epistle to Bathurst* provides a telling picture of the repercussions of the South Sea Bubble in 1720. While Pope doesn't forget the investors who lost everything, he bothers less about perpetrators in the financial industry than about the hypocrisy of a corrupt crew in government and parliament whose regulatory touch was so light as to be invisible.

For a long time *An Essay on Man* was about the most cited treatise worldwide on morals and metaphysics, while *An Essay on Criticism* wittily expounds—well, criticism. Pope's version of Homer remains among the few translations of a masterpiece to constitute a major work in its own right when converted to the host language. He also wrote superb prose, for example in his good-humoured but damning retorts to the scandalous publisher Edmund Curll.

In case you thought Pope sounds a bit remote, you might recall when you last heard someone use phrases like these: "To err is human, to forgive divine"; "Fools rush in where angels fear to tread"; "Hope springs eternal in the human breast"; "Who breaks a butterfly upon a wheel?"; "A little learning is a dangerous thing"; "Damn with faint praise." We owe them all to one man. These and many more have entered the stock of colloquial language, an idiom Pope learnt to utilize in sparkling poems that explore the full range of the human comedy.

PAT ROGERS is Distinguished University Professor, University of South Florida; editor *of The Major Works of Alexander Pope* for the Oxford World's Classics; and author of works on Swift, Defoe, Fielding, Johnson, Boswell, and Austen, among others.

Originally published on 21 May 2013 at http://blog.oup.com/2013/05/dire-offences-alexander-pope/

"A flag of one's own? Aimé Césaire between poetry and politics"

BY GREGSON DAVIS

"Davis ties together literature and politics to explore the complexities of Aimé Césaire's thought. The post is appropriately international in scope, and Davis effortlessly integrates a brief history of postcolonial history into his account. Davis's recollection of his personal encounters with Césaire only serves to underscore the author's deep engagement with the issues surrounding negritude and the legacy of colonialism."

—**TIMOTHY ALLEN,** Associate Editor, Reference, Oxford University Press

---

Aimé Césaire (1913–2008) has left behind an extraordinary dual legacy as eminent poet and political leader. Several critics have claimed to observe a contradiction between the vehement anticolonial stance expressed in his writings and his political practice. Criticism has focused on his support for the law of "departmentalization" (which incorporated the French Antilles, along with other overseas territories, as administrative "departments" within the French Republic) and his reluctance to lead his country to political independence. However, this perception of contradiction is misleading. A close reading of his poetic corpus and his published essays, such as the famous *Discourse on Colonialism*, supports an integrated view of his social thought and political practice.

While Césaire respected the sentiment of "national pride," he was more deeply committed to the project of restoring "black pride"—an idea that transcends the institution of a modern nation-state. When I interviewed him in Fort-de-France, the city of which he was mayor from 1945 until 1993, the first question he put to me on learning that I was a native of the Caribbean island of Antigua was: "Are Antiguans proud to be black?"

The key to arriving at a holistic view of Césaire's ideological position is to be found not only in his espousal of "negritude," but also in his quest to achieve genuine "decolonization." By his controversial support of departmental status, Césaire signaled early in his career that true decolonization should embrace not only the political and economic spheres (though he doubted Martinique's ability to successfully "go it alone," given the persistence of "neocolonialist" control of global markets), but also the domain of cultural values. The leaders of newly created independent African nation-states (such as the Senegalese, Leopold Senghor, his close friend from his student days in Paris; or Sekou Touré of Guinea, whom he celebrated in a lyric poem, "Guinée") chose to follow the path advocated by Ghana's Kwame Nkrumah in the slogan "Seek ye first the political kingdom." Césaire, on the other hand, understood in a very prescient way that "neocolonialism" meant that economic exploitation invariably persists even after the hoisting of a new national flag.

Decolonization and negritude were inseparable in Césaire's thinking. Both were ambitious projects for remaking ex-colonial Martinican society by reinstating pride among its people of color. As his signature poem, *Cahier d'un retour au pays natal* ("Journal of a Homecoming," in my English rendition) discloses, he saw negritude as an ongoing process of resurrecting a positive racial identity for peoples of African descent in the face of the degradation inflicted on them by European colonial powers. In this regard he shared the insight of the historian and political leader, the Trinidadian Eric Williams, that racism in its New World incarnation had been cooked up by the slave owners as a rationalization for enslavement of Africans. He therefore came to regard the Haitian Revolution, in which the slaves of the wealthy colony of Saint-Domingue (as Haiti was called under colonial French rule) successfully wrested power from their masters, as the historic crucible of negritude. As Césaire puts it in an arresting passage in the "Journal," Haiti was the place "where for the first time negritude stood up tall and straight and declared that it believed in its humanity."

For Césaire, then, negritude, as incarnated in the Haitian revolution, involves adopting a rebellious stance against the dehumanization of blacks. This theme is present in several of his plays, such as *A Tempest*, which explores the psychological complexity of the relationship between colonizer and colonized. In his brilliant recasting of Shakespeare's play, the monstrous figure of Caliban is transformed into an articulate, subjugated native who plots a successful rebellion against his repressive master, the European Prospero.

Césaire's dual agenda was, at bottom, "moral" in conception. His consistent goal, as poet and politician, was to promote genuine equality for the blacks of his homeland in the sphere of public policy no less than in social relations.

During his long service as deputy from Martinique to the French parliament, he acted as moral gadfly by making uncompromising "interventions" in order to ensure that the Antilles, as an "overseas department," received treatment equal to that of the departments in continental France. He continued to play this role even after his official retirement, most famously in his brush with the former French president, Nicolas Sarkozy: Césaire publicly rebuked Sarkozy after he made a notorious remark about the benefits of French colonialism. By an ironic twist of fate, Sarkozy eventually made up for his lapse on the occasion of Césaire's posthumous canonization in the French Panthéon by delivering a laudatory tribute to the great writer and statesman, in which he declared: "To tell the truth, he never ceased to goad France into examining its conscience" (My translation).

When I once asked him in a conversation in the mayor's office what he thought of the radical independence movement (then centered in the sister island of Guadeloupe), he replied: "The French do not want independence." Since the blacks of the French Caribbean were citizens of France, he was content to reaffirm the preference of the majority to retain their departmental status. For those who deplore this preference, I offer the following challenge: visit a few of the independent mini-states of the Caribbean archipelago and compare their economic and social progress with that of the Martinique bequeathed by the Césairean gadfly.

———

GREGSON DAVIS is Professor of Classics and Comparative Literature at New York University, where his research focuses on the interpretation of poetic texts in the Greco-Roman as well as Caribbean traditions. He has taught previously at Stanford University, Cornell University, and Duke University. His published work includes a biography of Aimé Césaire, translations of Césaire's poetry, and the entry on Césaire in *The Oxford Encyclopedia of African Thought*, available online at the *Oxford African American Studies Center.*

Originally published on 26 June 2013 at http://blog.oup.com/2013/06/aime-cesaire-poetry-politics/

"The G20: Policies, politics, and power"

BY MIKE BERRY

"The idea of revisiting a 'classic' with a mind to understanding the work in current context appeals. Published in 1958, John Kenneth Galbraith's *The Affluent Society* stayed on the bestseller list for six months and has never been out of print since. As with many iconic books that transcend the disciplinary boundaries of their author, it stimulated widespread interest and heated debate, but is now more often referred to rather than read. However Galbraith's critique of the orthodox economics of his day is, I believe, of continuing relevance, and such understandings are especially important in today's economic climate. Mike Berry looks back from the vantage point of the present to see how well Galbraith's analysis of affluence has fared in the intervening half-century. For the record, and as you'd expect, it covers inequality, insecurity, inflation, debt, consumer behaviour, financialization, the economic role of government ('social balance'), the power of ideas, the role of power in the economy, and the nature of the good society."

—**ADAM SWALLOW,** Commissioning Editor,
Economics and Finance, Oxford University Press

Five years after the worst economic crisis since the Great Depression, the world waits for recovery. Last time it took a world war and 40 million deaths to achieve. In 2008, a domino—Lehman Brothers—fell over, sparking a financial crisis that quickly threatened to bring the developed economies of the world crashing down. "This sucker could go down" was President George W. Bush's pithy summary. Only concerted and unprecedented action by the central banks and Treasury departments of the major countries and their smaller trading partners—now known as the G20—narrowly averted catastrophe. But it was a close-run, and we are not out of the woods yet, as the economies of Europe, Japan and North America struggle to grow, weighed down with public debt and under-capitalised banks. A pall of pessimism pervades government and financial markets.

The world appears topsy-turvy, like a Shakespearian scene from *Twelfth Night*, in which lord becomes servant and servant lord. The Western economies hang on the action or inaction of a small number of men and two women (Christine Lagarde and Angela Merkel), cloistered in the board rooms of the central banks, International Monetary Fund (IMF), and national governments. The captains of industry have been demoted, great companies drip-fed by whatever credit the "gnomes of Zurich," the predators of Wall Street, and the policy makers in Washington in their confused wisdom decree. In this upside down world, "fair is foul," as every suggestion of positive economic news about recovery in the real economy sends financial markets into panic. Addicted to the US Federal Reserves' money-printing regime, more politely termed "quantitative easing" (it sounds less inflationary), the markets take fright at any suggestion that the printing presses might slow down. In Europe, "austerity" has triumphed as the official mantra of the European Union. The "Washington Dissensus" has taken hold as "Austerians" battle with "Keynesians," replacing the easy neoliberal faith in efficient markets and fable of The Great Moderation. "All that is solid melts into air," as economists and policy makers scratch their heads in frustration. Nothing seems to be working.

None of this would have surprised twentieth-century American public intellectual Number One, John Kenneth Galbraith. An outsider who grew up in a small Canadian farming community, Galbraith retained this marginalised status in his chosen profession of economics. Eschewing the models, methods, and mathematics of modern economics, he devoted a long lifetime to attacking his colleagues in a prolific series of widely read books, the most famous of which was, of course, *The Affluent Society*, published in the first post-war period of American triumphalism. (The second period of American hubris occurred after the fall of communism in the "end of ideology" era of the 1990s, to be pricked by 9/11, the subsequent failures in Iraq and Afghanistan, and the outbreak of the global financial crisis.) Galbraith died two years before the fall of Lehman Brothers, but his lifetime's work would have prepared him for that event and for the muddled responses and blame shifting of both his colleagues and the bankers. Galbraith had written extensively on the nature of money and whence it came. He was deeply skeptical of the wisdom of the monetary authorities and the venality of actors in the financial sector. Like Keynes, he saw monetary policy as a weak reed on which to base economic recovery.

On re-reading Galbraith's book, the overwhelming truths that stand out for me in his critique of his society—and by extension, our own—amount to two. First, his famous construct—*the conventional wisdom*—has stood the test of time. Herd thinking and herd behaviour characterize us as a social species, in economics as everywhere. Being wrong in company is far preferable to being wrong alone, even if occasionally a stand against the wind proves to be right. It is the risk of being wrong alone that dissuades people, including economists, from seeking lonely ways of being right. Innovation is, as Galbraith observed about both politicians and businessmen, much lauded in principle but little embraced in practice; in later decades this insight was parodied in the mock warning of a fictional civil service chief to his political master: "That is very courageous, Minister." Ideas about our world that predominate are those that are generally accepted and acceptable. This last point raises Galbraith's other major point.

Policy is not just about disinterested scientific advice. *Policy is about politics and politics is about power.* Power is largely absent from orthodox economic accounts of how capitalist economies work. Even the limited use made of the concept—in models of imperfect competition—is ignored in the higher reaches of theory (exceptions, of course, exist) where the rarefied microfoundations of mainstream macroeconomics assume perfect or near-perfect markets. Throughout his career, Galbraith saw power, its genesis, application, and outcome as central to understanding the development of post-war American capitalism and the latter's export to the world. His view of the bifurcated nature of capitalism focused on the internal dynamics of corporate capitalism. His Presidential Address to the American Economic Association Conference in 1971, titled "Power in Economics," left little impact on a profession rapidly turning to a highly formalistic and politically naïve discipline practice.

Both insights help us begin to understand the current mess that the global economy is experiencing.

MIKE BERRY is Emeritus Professor at RMIT University, Melbourne, Australia, where he was for many years Professor of Urban Studies and Public Policy. He is the author of *The Affluent Society Revisited*. He is a frequent adviser to state and federal governments in Australia and has had visiting positions at a number of international institutions, including Rutgers University, Lund University, the University of Cambridge, and the University of Sussex.

Originally published on 17 December 2013 at http://blog.oup.com/2013/12/g20-policies-politics-power-economics/

"Q&A with Claire Payton on Haiti, spirituality, and oral history"

BY CAITLIN TYLER-RICHARDS

"In this piece, Claire Payton discusses the problems and possibilities of her oral history work in Haiti. She raises important issues concerning doing oral history outside of her native language, and the possibility of using oral history to give voice to the voiceless. The piece also touches on the ethics and responsibilities of doing oral history in the aftermath of disaster."

—TROY REEVES, OUPblog contributor and Managing Editor of the *Oral History Review*

About a month ago, when we celebrated the release of the *Oral History Review* Volume 40.2, we mentioned that one of the goals in putting together the issue was to expand the journal's geographical scope. Towards that end, we were excited to publish Claire Payton's "Vodou and Protestantism, Faith and Survival: The Contest over Spiritual Meaning of the 2010 Earthquake in Haiti." Hopefully, by now you have all had a chance to read Payton's article, in which she discusses the Haiti Memory Project and the spiritual dimension of everyday Haitians' testimony following the January 2010 earthquake. If not, be sure to have a look before or after you read my follow-up interview with the author.

The Haiti Memory Project (HMP) plays a large part in your article, so could you talk a bit more about how you came to the idea?

The idea for the HMP emerged from conversations I had with friends and colleagues in the weeks following the 2010 earthquake, about the possibilities and limitations of responding to a disaster like that from afar. There was a lot of talk in the media about what Haitians were experiencing and what they needed, but not much of it from Haitians themselves.

Of course. And do you—or others—plan to add to it in the future?

Over the past year, I have been overseeing follow-up interviews with some of the participants, which has provided another dimension to memories of disaster.

Excellent! As we see in your article, your work with the HMP has already led to some excellent insights on Haitian spirituality, the fluidity of which you suggest is especially visible in survivors' testimony. How did you come to this particular topic?

Honestly, I resisted writing about it for a while. Vodou in particular is often a gateway for essentializing, exotifying narratives about Haiti, so as a scholar I never had much interest in it. But it was hard not to recognize that tensions around spirituality and identity were practically omnipresent across the HMP interviews. They really just stood out to me, and I was being dishonest with myself by pretending otherwise. Then in late 2012 I went to Haiti as part of a research team for a UFL-Duke project called The Vodou Archive, and that basically served as a crash course in Haitian spiritual practices, taught by practitioners themselves. I felt more comfortable engaging with these issues after that.

Ah, okay. Somewhat related to that, could you talk a bit about conducting oral history research outside the United States and in a foreign language?

It was definitely a challenge, but it was also an opportunity. The native language in Haiti is Creole, while the language of government, education, and all things official is French. When I first went to Haiti, I was fluent in French but only spoke a smattering of Haitian Creole. I worked with translator-friends. I actually learned Haitian Creole through the interviewing process, through the hours and hours every day of sitting with people and listening to them very intently and then having their words translated into French.

I didn't always want to stop the flow of someone's steam of consciousness because I didn't understand and needed a translation, so I reminded myself that it was all being documented and that that was the whole point. I could listen to them again later. But going back and listening to my earliest interviews now, I see that this led me to put my foot in my mouth more than a few times and definitely shaped the relationships I established with participants. But not having optimal circumstances shouldn't be a reason not to do something you believe is important. You make do.

Wow, that sounds stressful.

Another complication is that Creole language transcriptions and translations are definitely harder to get done, and harder to get done right. I couldn't do them myself. I learned how to speak Creole, but I don't really know how to write it. Like I said, it's a challenge.

Speaking of challenges . . . Last December, I spoke with our Media Reviews Editor Jennifer Abraham Cramer about oral histories she collected following Hurricanes Rita and Katrina, and the unique position this research put her in. What was it like to collect interviews following the earthquake? Any strategies you took going in, or developed along the way? Do you have any advice for oral historians conducting research in the wake of natural disasters?

Everything in the interview seems like pretty great advice, especially if you are part of a team or institution that has support for things like psychological training. But what do you do if you are just an individual with little or no funding or institutional support? How can those kinds of projects be responsible and ethical too?

When considering these issues, I take solace in Alessandro Portelli's suggestion that oral history ethical guidelines are merely the formalization of the deeper spirit of oral history. While training is invaluable, it cannot replace an inner compass that guides many people to oral history in the first place. "Ultimately, in fact ethical and legal guidelines only make sense if they are the outward manifestation of a broader and deeper sense of personal and political commitment to honesty and truth" (Alessandro Portelli, "Trying to Gather a Little Knowledge," ***The Battle of Valle Giulia, 55)*****.**

I am by no means suggesting that people shouldn't educate themselves about best practices and adhere to them as much as possible. But I don't think that people should get discouraged from taking on difficult projects because they fear they can't execute them perfectly.

I can say, as someone who studies African History, that that is one mental obstacle I often have to overcome when thinking about field research, so thank you for that. And now, as per Troy's policy, we like to give the interviewee the last word. So, is there anything you'd like to add regarding the HMP or your article? Plugs for upcoming projects?

Just that in keeping with my goal of creating new narratives about Haiti, I am developing an oral history project based on the lives of influential Haitian women! I am also developing a dissertation on urban community histories in Port-au-Prince.

Exciting. We look forward to seeing the result of both projects. Thanks again for the article, and for chatting with me.

CAITLIN TYLER-RICHARDS was the Editorial/Media Assistant at the *Oral History Review*. When not sharing profound witticisms at @OralHistReview, Caitlin pursues a PhD in African History at the University of Wisconsin-Madison. Her research revolves around the intersection of West African history, literature and identity construction, as well as a fledgling interest in digital humanities. Before coming to Madison, Caitlin worked for the Lannan Center for Poetics and Social Practice at Georgetown University. CLAIRE PAYTON is a graduate student in the History Department at Duke University and creator of the Haiti Memory Project. She is the author of "Vodou and Protestantism, Faith and Survival: The Contest over Spiritual Meaning of the 2010 Earthquake in Haiti" in the latest issue of the *Oral History Review*.

Originally published on 20 December 2013 at http://blog.oup.com/2013/12/haiti-earthquake-oral-history-spirituality-vodou/

"Lucy in the scientific method"

BY TIM KASSER

"I love working with psychology content because it can take you in so many surprising directions. There's so much more to psychology than the proverbial couch! Take Tim Kasser, a professor of psychology at Knox College who studies materialism and consumer culture, among other things. Since Kasser was a teenager, he had dreamed of writing a biography of John Lennon, but it wasn't until two decades later that he was able to apply his expertise as a research psychologist and scientist—and shed his outlook as "fan"—towards a systematic investigation into understanding Lennon through his lyrics. In this piece, Kasser outlines his three-step process for understanding the meaning behind a song. His method is rigorous, but those who, like me, remember poring over liner notes in high school will appreciate the pursuit of interpreting the language of a beloved song."

—**ABBY GROSS,** Senior Editor, Psychology, Oxford University Press

---

Humans seem to love attempting to understand the meaning of songs. Back in my college days, I spent many hours talking with friends about what this or that song must mean. Nowadays, numerous websites are devoted to providing space for fans to dissect and share their interpretations of their favorite songs (e.g., Song Meanings, Song Facts, and Lyric Interpretations). There is even a webpage with a six-step program for understanding a song's meaning.

As a scientist and a psychologist, I usually find myself rather dissatisfied with the explanations I see on these sites, as well as the ones that my friends and I generated back in my youth. The explanations given often feel too simplistic, as though a single biographical fact could explain the whole scope of a song. They may also be based on an intuitive hunch, rather than good theorizing about why people create what they do. At other times, the interpreter seems to lose all sense of objectivity and instead projects his or her own concerns or issues onto the artist—I know I've been guilty of that one! Or the interpreter seems all too willing to accept the artist's own explanation for the song, when we know from a good deal of psychological research that people are not so good at explaining their own behaviors and motivations.

For the last decade or so, I've been trying to avoid these mistakes as I've attempted to understand John Lennon's "Lucy in the Sky with Diamonds." There are three standard explanations given for the meaning of the song, but each has its problems.

Probably the most popular explanation is that the song is about tripping on the drug LSD. Certainly Lennon did a lot of drugs around the time he wrote this song, and the initials of the song are the same as the drug.

> **Problem:** Lennon always denied that the song was about LSD, even though he admitted other songs (like "Tomorrow Never Knows") were about the drug. Why would he deny a drug reference in this case but not the others?

Another oft-repeated explanation for the song is that it is about a picture John Lennon's almost four-year-old son Julian gave him—a picture of Julian's friend Lucy, floating in the sky with diamonds. All I've read suggests that such a moment in time did indeed occur, and there is little doubt that Julian's picture does look like a girl floating in a diamond-filled sky.

> **Problem:** Why would this picture lead Lennon to write these lyrics, as opposed to some other lyrics? There are no "plasticine porters" or rivers or train stations in Julian's drawing.

Lennon's own explanation, shared a dozen years after he wrote the song, was that it was about his "dream girl," who turned out to be Yoko Ono, even though he hadn't met her yet. This is certainly a psychologically deeper explanation than any of the others.

> **Problem:** Why did Lennon deny that he knew Yoko at the time he wrote the song when his biography makes it clear they had met months earlier and had even eaten lunch at his house? And if she was his dream girl, why is Lucy constantly "gone" in the song?

Given my dissatisfaction with these explanations and the non-scientific approach to understanding a song's meaning that is so often used, I set about developing a three-step process that I hoped would provide a rigorous, scientifically based way of understanding "Lucy in the Sky with Diamonds." (Time will tell how well it works for other songs by other artists.)

Step 1: Derive a full description of the song.

Describing what needs to be studied is the first step any scientist must take when trying to explain any phenomenon. I therefore sought to describe the characteristics of this particular creative expression by adapting four established methods that other researchers had used in the past.

The first method I used was to run a linguistic word count program on the song. I then compared the results from "Lucy in the Sky with Diamonds" to other songs Lennon had written and other popular songs of the time. This helped me see the style in which Lennon had written the song.

The second method involved conducting a "scripting analysis" of "Lucy in the Sky with Diamonds" and Lennon's two earliest songs. This helped me to understand whether their narrative structures were similar (which would suggest a theme of long-standing concern for Lennon). I even had another psychologist, naïve to my purposes, derive a script.

An "association analysis" was the third method I used. For this, I mapped out the basic themes likely to have been on Lennon's mind when he chose the specific words he used in the song's lyrics. To this end, I reviewed all of his previous songs to see how he had earlier used each of the words that made up "Lucy in the Sky with Diamonds."

For the fourth method, I applied a similar method as the third to identify the musical idioms and structures that Lennon used in the song to identify the previous two songs that were most musically similar to "Lucy in the Sky with Diamonds." I thought doing so might tell me what was on Lennon's mind when he chose the particular melody, key, etc., that he used in "Lucy in the Sky with Diamonds."

Thus, by the end of this first step, I had obtained a relatively objective, multi-faceted, and multi-theoretical description of the song Lennon had created in the winter of 1966–67.

Step 2: Understand the context of the song's creation.

Why had this man written this song at this time of his life? I read biographies to better understand Lennon's formative experiences (such as his early life and adolescence), the stresses he had recently been under (such as death threats), the drugs he recently had been taking (LSD), and the "activating event" that had spurred this particular creative act (i.e., Julian's drawing). I then connected these data to relevant psychological and empirical literatures, such as attachment theory, grief research, and what we know about the effects of massive doses of LSD on the mind.

At the end of this step, I had obtained a sense of who Lennon was, what he'd been going through recently, and what spurred him on to this particular creation. At this point I could hazard an explanation of what I thought the song was about.

Step 3: Test my explanation by looking at songs Lennon wrote next.

I decided to test my explanation by examining the songs that Lennon wrote in the three years after "Lucy in the Sky with Diamonds." I was particularly interested to see whether Lennon continued to express the themes that seemed to have led to the creation of "Lucy in the Sky with Diamonds" when, later in his life, he experienced stresses and situations similar to the ones he had gone through in 1966 and early 1967.

In closing, some might argue that this kind of scientific approach to understanding the meaning of a song is too objective, and too clinical, that it robs artistic creations of their mystery and magic. Other researchers who use the scientific method in the realm of human experience (e.g., religion, life, cosmology) have certainly received similar critiques of their work.

Nonetheless, I continue to hold that if someone really wants to know what a song might mean, there is no better approach than to apply the methods of science in a rigorous, systematic, and theoretically informed way.

I also have the sense that the understanding that comes from this process does not rob the song of its beauty or meaning. Knowing the science behind sunsets hasn't made me less awed by their beauty, and understanding what was on Lennon's mind when he wrote "Lucy in the Sky with Diamonds" has not made me think any less of the song. Indeed, just the opposite.

TIM KASSER is Professor of Psychology at Knox College. His publications include *Lucy in the Mind of Lennon*, *The High Price of Materialism*, and many scientific articles and book chapters. Tim enjoys playing the piano (including the blues and songs by the Beatles), interpreting dreams, and spending time with his family at their home in the western Illinois countryside.

Originally published on 13 February 2014 at http://blog.oup.com/2014/02/lennon-lucy-sky-diamonds-scientific-analysis/

"Neanderthals may have helped East Asians adapting to sunlight"

BY QILIANG DING AND YA HU

"This article in *Molecular Biology and Evolution* highlights how advances in genome sequencing, as well the analysis of ancient DNA, is helping to enhance our understanding not only of evolution but of our human history. The authors present evidence that the co-existence of Neanderthals with early humans during their migration out of Africa may have helped East Asian populations adapt to sunlight exposure. Where we come from and how we've developed as a species is a truly fascinating field of study, and as the science becomes more sophisticated we can uncover insights such as this which give an incredibly evocative peek into our past. "

—**JENNIFER BOYD,** Publisher, Journals, Oxford University Press

---

Hominins and their closest living relative, chimpanzees, diverged approximately 6.5 million years ago on the African continent. Fossil evidence suggests that hominins have migrated away from Africa at least twice since then. Crania of the first wave of migrants, such as Neanderthals in Europe and Peking Man in East Asia, show distinct morphological features that are different from contemporary humans (also known as *Homo sapiens sapiens*). The first wave of migration was estimated to have occurred 7–9 million years ago. In the 1990s, studies on

Y-chromosome and mitochondrial DNA proved that the contemporary Eurasians are descendants of the second wave of migrants, who migrated out of Africa less than 100,000 years ago.

It has been reported that the habitats of Neanderthals and ancestors of contemporary Eurasians overlapped both in time and space, and therefore provides possibility of introgression between Neanderthals and ancestors of Eurasians. This possibility is confirmed by recent studies, which suggest that about 1–4% of Eurasian genomes are from Neanderthal introgression.

Adaptation to local environment is crucial for newly-arrived migrants, and the process of local adaptation is sometimes time-consuming. Since Neanderthals arrived in Eurasia ten times earlier than ancestors of Eurasians, we are trying to figure out whether the Neanderthal introgressions helped the ancestors of Eurasians adapt to the local environment.

Our study reports that Neanderthal introgressive segments on chromosome 3 may have helped East Asians adapting to the intensity of ultraviolet-B (UV-B) irradiation in sunlight. We call the region containing the Neanderthal introgression the "*HYAL*" region, as it contains three genes that encode hyaluronoglucosaminidases.

We first noticed that the entire *HYAL* region is included in an unusually large linkage disequilibrium (LD) block in East Asian populations. Such a large LD block is a typical signature of positive natural selection. More interestingly, it is observed that some Eurasian haplotypes at the *HYAL* region show a closer relationship to the Neanderthal haplotype than to the contemporary African haplotypes, implicating recent Neanderthal introgression. We confirmed the Neanderthal introgression in *HYAL* region by employing a series of statistical and population genetic analyses.

Further, we examined whether the *HYAL* region was under positive natural selection using two published statistical tests. Both suggest that the *HYAL* region was under positive natural selection and pinpoint a set of single nucleotide polymorphisms (SNPs) contributed by Neanderthal introgression as the candidate targets of positive natural selection.

We then explored the potential functional importance of Neanderthal introgression in the *HYAL* region. The *HYAL* genes attracted our attention, as they are important in hyaluronan metabolism and cellular response to UV-B irradiation. We noticed that an SNP pinpointed as a potential target for positive natural selection was located in the most conservative exon of the *HYAL2* gene. We suspect that this SNP (known as rs35455589) may have altered the function of the *HYAL2* protein, since this SNP is also associated with the risk of keloid, a dermatological disorder related to hyaluronan metabolism.

Next, we interrogated the global distribution of Neanderthal introgression at the *HYAL* region. It is observed that the Neanderthal introgression reaches a very high frequency in East Asian populations, which ranges from 49.4% in Japanese to 66.5% in Southern Han Chinese. The frequency of Neanderthal introgression is higher in southern East Asian populations compared to northern East Asian populations. Such evidence might suggest latitude-dependent selection, which implicates the role of UV-B intensity.

We discovered that Neanderthal introgression on chromosome 3 was under positive natural selection in East Asians. We also found that a gene (*HYAL2*) in the introgressive region is related to the cellular response to UV-B, and an allele from Neanderthal introgression may have altered the function of HYAL2.

As such, we think it is possible that Neanderthals may have helped East Asians to adapt to sunlight.

QILIANG DING and YA HU are MSc students at the Institute of Genetics at Fudan University and Intern Students at the CAS-MPG Partner Institute of Computational Biology of the Chinese Academy of Sciences. Their research interest lies in revealing evolutionary history of hominids using ancient and contemporary human genomes. They are the authors of the paper “Neanderthal Introgression at Chromosome 3p21.31 Was Under Positive Natural Selection in East Asians,” which appears in the journal *Molecular Biology and Evolution*.

Originally published on 3 March 2014 at http://blog.oup.com/2014/03/neanderthals-may-have-helped-east-asians-adapting-to-sunlight/

"Thinking more about our teeth"

BY PETER S. UNGAR

"Being in the Pam Ayres school of dental hygiene, I often find myself thinking of teeth. This is a lovely little piece that covers a great deal (as do all the VSIs) (*slugs have teeth*?!) and made me want to read the whole book, so I can appreciate the small miracle of those (in my case) much neglected molars and canines."

—LUCIANA O'FLAHERTY, Publisher, Global Academic Business, and Very Short Introductions series editor, Oxford University Press

---

Most of us only think about teeth when something's wrong with them—when they come in crooked, break, or begin to rot. But take a minute to consider your teeth as the extraordinary feat of engineering they are. They concentrate and transmit the forces needed to break food, again and again, up to millions of times over a lifetime. And they do it without themselves being broken in the process—with the very same raw materials used to make the plants and animals being eaten.

Chewing is like a perpetual death match in the mouth, with plants and animals developing tough or hard tissues for protection, and teeth evolving ways to sharpen or strengthen themselves to overcome those defenses. Most living things don't want to be eaten. They often protect themselves by reinforcing their parts to stop eaters from breaking them into small enough bits to swallow or digest. It could be a hard shell to keep a crack from starting, or tough fibers to keep one from spreading. Either way, the eater still has to eat. And that's where teeth come in. The variety of tooth types, especially across the mammals, is extraordinary. It's a testament to what evolution can accomplish given time, motive, and opportunity.

Lots of animals have "teeth"; sea urchins, spiders, and slugs all have hardened tissues used for food acquisition and processing. But *real* teeth, like yours and mine, are special. They first appeared half a billion years ago, and Nature has spent the whole time since tinkering with ways to make them better. It's a story written in stone—the fossil record. We see the appearance of a hard, protective coating of enamel, better ways of attaching tooth to jaw, differentiation of front and back teeth, tighter fit between opposing surfaces, and a new joint for precise movements of the jaw.

The motive is *endothermy*; we mammals heat our bodies from within. And chewing allows us to squeeze the energy we need to fuel our furnaces. The opportunity is evolvability; very slight genetic tweaks can have dramatic effects on tooth form and function. Consider the incredible variety of different tooth types in mammals, matched so well to the foods individual species eat. A lion has sharp-crested chewing teeth, with blades opposing one another like a pair of scissors, for slicing flesh. A cow has broad, flat ones broken by thin, curved ridges, like a cheese grater, for milling grass. You and I have thick molars with rounded cusps that fit neatly into opposing basins, like a mortar and pestle, for crushing and grinding whatever it is we eat.

There can be little doubt that the diversity, abundance, and success of mammals, including us, are due, in no small measure, to our teeth. Look in a mirror, smile, and think about it.

PETER S. UNGAR received his PhD in Anthropological Sciences from Stony Brook University and taught gross anatomy in the medical schools at Johns Hopkins and Duke before moving to the University of Arkansas, where he now serves as Distinguished Professor and Chairman of the Department of Anthropology. He has written or co-authored more than 125 scientific papers on ecology and evolution for books and journals and is the author of *Teeth: A Very Short Introduction*.

Originally published on 14 March 2014 at http://blog.oup.com/2014/03/thinking-more-about-our-teeth/

"Kathleen J. Pottick on Superstorm Sandy and social work resources"

"This brief interview encapsulates, in so many different ways, what we are all about. Here we have a social work professor who was herself impacted directly by Hurricane Sandy, forming a university-community-agency initiative designed to ensure that practitioners in the field had the information they needed in order to effectively serve their clients and communities. The product itself, the *Encyclopedia of Social Work* (ESW), is intended to do just that—to provide authoritative, up-to-date information to scholars, students, and practitioners *where they are*, and Prof. Pottick worked with partners at OUP, Rutgers, and local agencies to make this happen. It's just a great story that shows what social workers do, how an online encyclopedia can provide a valuable service in the age of Wikipedia, and the real impact that a scholarly press can have on people in need within our own community."

—**DANA BLISS**, Senior Editor, Social Work, Oxford University Press

---

Rutgers University explored options to offer funding and training programs to assist clients who were hit hard by Superstorm Sandy. One of their more recent initiatives provided subscriptions to the *Encyclopedia of Social Work Online* to seven agency directors who needed access to scholarly research to guide their work in the field. We spoke to Kathleen Pottick, professor in

Rutgers University's School of Social Work, who spearheaded this endeavor to hear the story behind their work.

How did the Rutgers grant for this project come about?

While we were struggling—as a university, as a community, as a state—to recover from Superstorm Sandy in October 2012, our development director recognized an opportunity for funding through foundations supporting Sandy relief efforts in New Jersey. We knew that our students were in field agencies throughout the state serving those directly impacted by the storm, and we wanted to give those students the tools to help those surviving this natural disaster. Many of our survivors were newly needy, and our students had to be trained in dealing with this population.

We believed there might be private foundation backing to develop training programs because they would have an immediate, concrete effect on helping clients. After we received interest from a foundation, several key faculty and staff sat together to map the best strategy that would make the largest impact in our state. We presented our proposal within the week, and they gave us a budget to implement this disaster training and service work.

What was your initial aim?

Our initial aim was to respond quickly to this disaster to assist victims of the event, while, for the first time, integrating graduate social work students into disaster-related clinical and non-profit organization management agencies through field placements. We wanted students quickly to be able to provide concrete services, as well as directed mental health counseling.

How will this work support future goals at the School of Social Work?

Students participating in the program were called Disaster Fellows and given supplemental training on disaster response and disaster mental health counseling, in addition to their usual advanced social work training. They applied their training through supervised field placements, mostly in nontraditional, newly developed agency locations, and we now have a base of alumni who can take those skills to their professional agencies throughout the state, and beyond. There are opportunities to present our work at national and regional conferences to ensure the human experience is not overlooked, as environmentalists and climatologists discuss Sandy's impact. The school will continue to enhance its reputation within the university as an integral collaborator on current issues, as well as a leader in innovative responses to disaster.

How did you and Cynthia Franklin, Editor of *Encyclopedia of Social Work* online, come together to start discussing your plans? Why did you select *Encyclopedia of Social Work* to assist the research of these individuals?

It was important that our agency partners continued to feel support from the School of Social Work as they continued to serve clients in their communities, especially for long-term effects of the Sandy disaster, after our original students were gone. We wanted those agencies to have the most current and comprehensive information at their fingertips. The *Encyclopedia of Social Work* was the first place we went because we knew that the continuous online update function, with links to relevant articles and journals, would be most effective for these partner agencies. Our partners could easily search for specific, up-to-the-minute information without thumbing through pages of a static text.

When we told agency directors that they would have access to the *Encyclopedia*, they were extremely appreciative. The director of the Mental Health Association of New Jersey said, "The *Encyclopedia* will help us tremendously with our ongoing efforts to enhance the education and training of our recovery community as we continue to work with the survivors of Hurricane Sandy who require ongoing attention. We will also use this resource in Mental Health First-Aid and other disaster-related trainings that are conducted throughout New Jersey."

Another community agency director stated, "This subscription will be one more useful tool in our 'resource toolbox' to have on hand when assisting individuals and families who have been exposed to a traumatic life event such as Hurricane Sandy and who need professional guidance."

For readers not residing in this part of the country, can you elaborate on how and why Sandy was particularly catastrophic for New Jersey residents?

Sandy caused unprecedented havoc across a broad swath of the Middle Atlantic region of the United States, and unlike normal storms, its hurricane-force winds did not dissipate quickly once the storm got over land, but extended approximately 100 miles inland. People who had never experienced hardship in their lives were drastically affected, and in New Jersey, many of the survivors of this storm lived in middle- and upper-class areas. A very large number of residents were seeking help from local agencies for the first time. They didn't know what resources were available to them, nor did they understand the effects this disaster would have on them for months and years to come. In some areas of the state, entire communities were destroyed, and survivors from them had to relocate completely, leaving not just their physical residence, but their neighbors, stores, resources, and their general sense of community. The theme for this year's National Social Work month, All People Matter, is quite relevant to us in New Jersey because we have stood together and have shown great resiliency as our communities rebuild.

In your opinion, what challenges are social workers facing in the current workforce? What about in education or research settings?

It is not specific challenges, but rather the breadth of them, that poses the major difficulty for the current social work workforce in serving not just traditionally vulnerable families and children, but newly needy classes of clients—be it in responding to increasingly common and devastating natural events, stagnant middle-class income, or the growing maze of governmental programs such as the Affordable Care Act. Interdisciplinary collaborations have become necessary so that social workers can function as parts of teams providing coordinated responses that require multiple interventions. Education is necessary to provide them with these skills, and research is necessary to understand the effectiveness of delivery mechanisms.

What are your goals for the coming year? Is this investment in the *Encyclopedia of Social Work* to social agencies just the beginning?

We hope to continue to educate our social work students in disaster work. Through our grant we developed training modules and coursework that can be replicated for interested students in the future. Our goal is to present our work and serve as a model for other workgroups when responding to disaster. Many organizations focus on the physical clean-up process, post-disaster —the debris, the remediation, the coastline. But we want to have social work serve as the helping profession that not only assists people coping with immediate tangible needs, but also that brings awareness to the mental and emotional issues that survivors face, and prepares them for potential future ones.

Any final thoughts?

Universities and non-profit organizations are strategically poised to reach out to philanthropic organizations for financial resources to invest in training a competent workforce for new special areas needing immediate attention. The investment in the *Encyclopedia of Social Work* for agencies working in the new areas is critical for long-term practice effects.

KATHLEEN J. POTTICK is a professor in Rutgers University's School of Social Work and Core Senior Faculty at Rutgers' Institute for Health, Health Care Policy and Aging Research. She has served in a variety of administrative roles in the School of Social Work, including Acting Dean (2011–2013) and Associate Dean for Faculty Development (2009–2011).

Originally published on 18 March 2014 at http://blog.oup.com/2014/03/superstorm-sandy-social-work-resources/

"'You can't wear that here'"

BY ANDREW HAMBLER AND IAN LEIGH

"Legal topics are often a little inaccessible, meaning that a blog post uses up several paragraphs just explaining what the problem is. Here, the title ('You can't wear that here') and the first sentence ('When a religious believer wears a religious symbol to work can their employer object?') immediately locate the issue for the reader, leaving the rest of the article to explain the state of play and future direction of the law on wearing religious symbols in the workplace. At the time of the legal judgment that this post examines, newspapers had to try to summarise the case in terms of somebody winning or losing, while specialist legal blogs debated the judgment's significance for specific Articles of the European Convention on Human Rights. The OUPblog piece managed to provide an accessible but nuanced explanation of the legal principles and findings yet also set out the judgment's significance in one pithy sentence: 'The idea that employees must leave their religion at the door has been dealt a decisive blow.'"

—**JOHN LOUTH,** Editor-in-Chief, Academic Law Books, Journals, and Online, Oxford University Press

---

When a religious believer wears a religious symbol to work can their employer object? The question brings corporate dress codes and expressions of religious belief into sharp conflict. The employee can marshal discrimination and human rights law on the one side, whereas the employer may argue that conspicuous religion makes for bad business.

The issue reached the European Court of Human Rights in 2013 in a group of cases (*Eweida and Others v. United Kingdom*), following a lengthy and unsuccessful domestic legal campaign, brought by a group of employees who argued that their right of freedom of religion and belief (under Article 9 of the Convention) had not been protected when the UK courts favoured their employers' interests.

Nadia Eweida, an airline check-in clerk, and Shirley Chaplin, a nurse, had been refused permission by their respective employers, British Airways and an NHS trust, to wear a small cross on a necklace so that it was visible to other people. The employer's rationale in each case was rather different. British Airways wanted to maintain a consistent corporate image so that no "customer-facing staff" should be permitted to wear jewellery for any reason. The NHS trust argued that there was a potential health and safety risk if jewellery were worn by nursing staff—in Ms. Chaplin's case, a disturbed patient might "seize the cross" and harm either themselves or indeed Ms. Chaplin.

Both applicants argued that their sense of religious obligation to wear a cross outweighed the employer's normal discretion in setting a uniform policy. They also argued that their respective employers had also been inconsistent because their uniform policies made a number of specific accommodations for members of minority faiths, such as Muslims and Sikhs.

A major difficulty for both Eweida and Chaplin was the risk that their cross-wearing could be dismissed as a personal preference rather than a protected manifestation of their beliefs. After all many—probably most—Christians do not choose to wear the cross. The UK domestic courts found that the practice was not regarded as a mandatory religious practice (applying a so-called "necessity" test) but rather one merely "motivated" by religion and not therefore eligible for protection. This did not help either Eweida or Chaplin, as both believed passionately that they had an obligation to wear the cross to attest to their faith (in Chaplin's case this was in response to a personal vow to God). The other major difficulty for both applicants was that the Court had also historically accepted a rather strange argument that people voluntarily surrender their right to freedom of religion and belief in the workplace when they enter into an employment contract, and so the employer has discretion to set its policies without regard to interfering with its employees' religious practices. If an employee found this too burdensome, then he or she could protect their rights by resigning and finding another job. This argument, ignoring the realities of the labour market and imposing a very heavy burden on religious employees, has been a key reason why so few "workplace" claims have been successful before the European Court.

Arguably, the most significant aspect of the judgment was that the religious liberty questions were in fact considered by the Court rather than being dismissed as being inapplicable in the workplace (as the government and the National Secular Society had both argued). The Court specifically repudiated both the necessity test and the doctrine of "voluntary surrender" of Article 9 rights at work. As a result, it has opened the door both to applications for protection for a much wider group of religious practices in the future and for claims relating to employment. From a religious liberty perspective, this is surely something to welcome.

Nadia Eweida's application was successful on its merits. It is now clear, therefore, that an employer cannot override the religious conscience of its staff due to the mere desire for uniformity. However, Chaplin was unsuccessful, the Court essentially finding that "health and safety" concerns provided a legitimate interest allowing the employer to override religious manifestation. This is disappointing, particularly since evidence was presented that the health and safety risks of a nurse wearing a cross were minimal and that, in this case, Chaplin was prepared to compromise to reduce them still further. Hopefully this aspect of the judgment (unnecessary deference to national authorities in the realm of health and safety) will be revisited in future.

Whether that happens or not, it is clear that religious expressions in the workplace now need to be approached differently after the European Court's ruling. The idea that employees must leave their religion at the door has been dealt a decisive blow. From now on, if corporate policy overrides employees' religious beliefs, then employers will be under a much greater obligation to demonstrate why, if at all, this is necessary.

———

ANDREW HAMBLER and IAN LEIGH are the authors of "Religious Symbols, Conscience, and the Rights of Others" in the *Oxford Journal of Law and Religion*. Dr. Andrew Hambler is senior lecturer in human resources and employment law at the University of Wolverhampton. His research focusses on how the manifestation of religion in the workplace is regulated both at an organisational and at a legal level. He is the author of *Religious Expression in the Workplace and the Contested Role of Law*. Ian Leigh is a Professor of Law at Durham University. He has written extensively on legal and human rights questions concerning religious liberty. He is the co-author, with Rex Ahdar, of *Religious Freedom in the Liberal State.*

Originally published on 26 March 2014 at http://blog.oup.com/2014/03/corporate-dress-code-expression-religious-belief/

"Does the 'serving-first advantage' actually exist?"

BY FRANC KLAASSEN AND JAN R. MAGNUS

"As a fan of both sport and statistics, this post drew me in from the start. The Moneyball phenomenon is yet to hit tennis in force, and this post hints at the potential that lies within the incredible dataset the authors created for their book. However, the post equally highlights how statistics can be misrepresentative and the dangers faced when they are interrogated closely. I hope Andy Murray has read this blog!"

—**CHRISTOPHER REID,** Editor, Medical Books and Journals, Oxford University Press

---

Suppose you are watching a tennis match between Novak Djokovic and Rafael Nadal. The commentator says: "Djokovic serves first in the set, so he has an advantage." Why would this be the case? Perhaps because he is then "always" one game ahead, thus serving under less pressure. But does it actually influence him and, if so, how?

Now we come to the seventh game, which some consider to be the most important game in the set. But is it? Nadal serves an ace at break point down (30-40). Of course! Real champions win the big points, but they win most points on service anyway. At first, it may appear that real champions outperform on big points, but it turns out that weaker players underperform, so that it only seems that the champions outperform. And Nadal goes on to win three consecutive games. He is in a winning mood, the momentum is on his side. But does a "winning mood" actually exist in tennis? (Spoiler: It does, but it is smaller than many expect.)

To figure out whether the "serving-first advantage" actually exists, we can use data on more than 1,000 sets played at Wimbledon in order to calculate how often the player who served first also won the set. This statistic shows that for the men there is a slight advantage in the first set, but no advantage in the other sets.

On the contrary, in the other sets, there is actually a disadvantage: the player who serves first in the set is more likely to lose the set than to win it. This is surprising. Perhaps it is different for the women? But no, the same pattern occurs in the women's singles.

It so happens that the player who serves first in a set (if it is not the first set) is usually the weaker player. This is so, because (a) the stronger player is more likely to win the previous set, and (b) the previous set is more likely won by serving the set out rather than by breaking serve. Therefore, the stronger player typically wins the previous set on service, so that the weaker player serves first in the next set. The weaker player is more likely to lose the current set as well, not because of a service (dis)advantage, but because he or she is the weaker player.

This example shows that we must be careful when we try to draw conclusions based on simple statistics. The fact that the player who serves first in the second and subsequent sets often loses the set is true, but this primarily concerns weaker players, while the original hypothesis includes all players. Therefore, we must control for quality differences, and statistical models enable us to do that properly. It then becomes clear that there is no advantage or disadvantage for the player who serves first in the second or subsequent sets; but it does matter in the first set, so it is wise to elect to serve after winning the toss.

———

FRANC KLAASSEN is Professor of International Economics at University of Amsterdam. JAN R. MAGNUS is Emeritus Professor at Tilburg University and Visiting Professor of Econometrics at the Vrije Universiteit Amsterdam. They are the co-authors of *Analyzing Wimbledon: The Power of Statistics.*

Originally published on 1 July 2014 at http://blog.oup.com/2014/07/wimbledon-tennis-serving-first-advantage/

"Transparency at the Fed"

BY RICHARD S. GROSSMAN

"I like this post because the writing is punchy, in contrast to a lot of academic writing—including my own—that is ponderous. It is also timely, as central bank behavior and practices are—and will continue to be—a hot topic in the coming months. Finally, I like it because it uses history to illuminate an issue of contemporary policy, one of my favorite approaches."

—**RICHARD S. GROSSMAN,** OUPblog columnist and the author of *Wrong*

As an early stage graduate student in the 1980s, I took a summer off from academia to work at an investment bank. One of my most eye-opening experiences was discovering just how much effort Wall Street devoted to "Fed watching," that is, trying to figure out the Federal Reserve's monetary policy plans.

If you spend any time following the financial news today, you will not find that surprising. Economic growth, inflation, stock market returns, and exchange rates, among many other things, depend crucially on the course of monetary policy. Consequently, speculation about monetary policy frequently dominates the financial headlines.

Back in the 1980s, the life of a Fed watcher was more challenging: not only were the Fed's future actions unknown, its current actions were also something of a mystery.

You read that right. Thirty years ago, not only did the Fed not tell you where monetary policy was going but, aside from vague statements, it did not say much about where it was either.

Given that many of the world's central banks were established as private, profit-making institutions with little public responsibility, and even less public accountability, it is unremarkable that central bankers became accustomed to conducting their business behind closed doors. Montagu Norman, the governor of the Bank of England between 1920 and 1944, was famous for the measures he would take to avoid the press. He adopted cloak-and-dagger methods, going so far as to travel under an assumed name, to avoid drawing unwanted attention to himself.

The Federal Reserve may well have learned a thing or two from Norman during its early years. The Fed's monetary policymaking body, the Federal Open Market Committee (FOMC), was created under the Banking Act of 1935. For the first three decades of its existence, it published brief summaries of its policy actions only in the Fed's annual report. Thus, policy decisions might not become public for as long as a year after they were made.

Limited movements toward greater transparency began in the 1960s. By the mid-1960s, policy actions were published 90 days after the meetings in which they were taken; by the mid-1970s, the lag was reduced to approximately 45 days.

Since the mid-1990s, the increase in transparency at the Fed has accelerated. The lag time for the release of policy actions has been reduced to about three weeks. In addition, minutes of the discussions leading to policy actions are also released, giving Fed watchers additional insight into the reasoning behind the policy.

More recently, the FOMC publicly announces its target for the Federal Funds rate, a key monetary policy tool, and explains its reasoning for the particular policy course chosen. Since 2007, the FOMC minutes include the numerical forecasts generated by the Federal Reserve's staff economists. And, in a move that no doubt would have appalled Montagu Norman, since 2011 the Federal Reserve chair has held regular press conferences to explain its most recent policy actions.

The Fed is not alone in its move to become more transparent. The European Central Bank, in particular, has made transparency a stated goal of its monetary policy operations. The Bank of Japan and Bank of England have made similar noises, although exactly how far individual central banks can, or should, go in the direction of transparency is still very much debated.

Despite disagreements over how much transparency is desirable, it is clear that the steps taken by the Fed have been positive ones. Rather than making the public and financial professionals waste time trying to figure out what the central bank plans to do—which, back in the 1980s, took a lot of time and effort and often led to incorrect guesses—the Fed just tells us. This makes monetary policy more certain and, therefore, more effective.

Greater transparency also reduces uncertainty and the risk of violent market fluctuations based on incorrect expectations of what the Fed will do. Transparency makes Fed policy more credible and, at the same time, pressures the Fed to adhere to its stated policy. And when circumstances force the Fed to deviate from the stated policy or undertake extraordinary measures, as it has done in the wake of the financial crisis, it allows it to do so with a minimum of disruption to financial markets.

Montagu Norman is no doubt spinning in his grave. But increased transparency has made us all better off.

RICHARD S. GROSSMAN is a Professor of Economics at Wesleyan University in Connecticut, and a visiting scholar at Harvard University's Institute for Quantitative Social Science. His most recent book is *WRONG: Nine Economic Policy Disasters and What We Can Learn from Them*. His homepage is RichardSGrossman.com, he blogs at UnsettledAccount.com, and you can follow him on Twitter at @RSGrossman.

Originally published on 6 August 2014 at http://blog.oup.com/2014/08/transparency-federal-reserve/

"Publishing tips from a journal editor: Selecting the right journal"

BY R. MICHAEL ALVAREZ

"Of the various blog posts I've done, I think this one is the most generally interesting. It provides some much-needed advice from the perspective of a journal editor about the matching problem that plagues many academic writers (not just in political science, but across the humanities and sciences). I also have found that authors hunger for honest guidelines about how to try to publish their material, and I believe that this post provides that perspective."

—R. MICHAEL ALVAREZ, OUPblog contributor and Co-Editor of *Political Analysis*

One of the most common questions that scholars confront is trying to find the right journal for their research papers. When I go to conferences, often I am asked: "How do I know if *Political Analysis* is the right journal for my work?"

This is an important question, in particular for junior scholars who don't have a lot of publishing experience—and for scholars who are nearing important milestones (like contract renewal, tenure, and promotion). In a publishing world where it may take months for an author to receive an initial decision from a journal, and then many additional months if they need to revise and resubmit their work to one or more subsequent journals, selecting the most appropriate journal can be critical for professional advancement.

So how can a scholar try to determine which journal is right for their work?

The first question an author needs to ask is how suitable their paper is for a particular journal. When I meet with my graduate students, and we talk about potential publication outlets for their work, my first piece of advice is that they should take a close look at the last three or four issues of the journals they are considering. I'll recommend that they look at the subjects that each journal is focusing on, including both substantive topics and methodological approaches. I also tell them to look closely at how the papers appearing in those journals are structured and how they are written (for example, how long the papers typically are, and how many tables and figures they have). The goal is to find a journal that is currently publishing papers that are most closely related to the paper that the student is seeking to publish, as assessed by the substantive questions typically published, the methodological approaches generally used, paper framing, and manuscript structure.

Potential audience is the second consideration. Different journals have different readers— meaning that authors can have some control over who might be exposed to their paper when they decide which journals to target for their work. This is particularly true for authors who are working on highly interdisciplinary projects, where they might be able to frame their paper for publication in related but different academic fields. In my own work on voting technology, for example, some of my recent papers have appeared in journals that have their primary audience in computer science, while others have appeared in more typical political science journals. So authors need to decide in many cases which audience they want to appeal to, and make sure that when they submit their work to a journal that appeals to that audience, the paper is written in an appropriate manner for that journal.

However, most authors will want to concentrate on journals in a single field. For those papers, a third question arises: whether to target a general interest journal or a more specialized field journal. This is often a very subjective question, as it is quite hard to know prior to submission whether a particular paper will be interesting to the editors and reviewers of a general interest journal. As general interest journals often have higher impact factors (I'll say more about impact factors next), many authors will be drawn to submit their papers to general interest journals even if that is not the best strategy for their work. Many authors will "start high," that is begin with general interest journals, and then once the rejection letters pile up, they will move to the more specialized field journals. While this strategy is understandable (especially for authors who are nearing promotion or tenure deadlines), it may also be counterproductive—the author will likely face a long and frustrating process getting their work published, if they submit first to general interest journals, get the inevitable rejections, and then move to specialized field journals. Thus, my advice (and my own practice with my work) is to avoid that approach, and to be realistic about the appeal of the particular research paper. That is, if your paper is going to appeal only to readers in a narrow segment of your discipline, then send it to the appropriate specialized field journal.

A fourth consideration is the journal's impact factor. Impact factors are playing an increasingly important role in many professional decisions, and they may be a consideration for many authors. Clearly, an author should generally seek to publish their work in journals that have higher impact than those that are lower impact. But again, authors should try to be realistic about their work, and make sure that regardless of the journal's impact factor, their submission is appropriate for the journal they are considering.

Finally, authors should always seek the input of their faculty colleagues and mentors if they have questions about selecting the right journal. And in many fields, journal editors, associate editors, and members of the journal's editorial board will often be willing to give an author some quick and honest advice about whether a particular paper is right for their journal. While many editors shy away from giving prospective authors advice about a potential submission, giving authors some brief and honest advice can actually save the editor and the journal a great deal of time. It may be better to save the author (and the journal) the time and effort that might get sunk into a paper that has little chance at success in the journal, and help guide the author to a more appropriate journal.

Selecting the right journal for your work is never an easy process. All scholars would like to see their work published in the most widely read and highest impact factor journals in their field. But very few papers end up in those journals, and authors can get their work into print more quickly and with less frustration if they first make sure their paper is appropriate for a particular journal.

R. MICHAEL ALVAREZ is Editor-in-Chief, along with Jonathan N. Katz, of *Political Analysis*.

Originally published on 17 August 2014 at http://blog.oup.com/2014/08/publishing-tips-journal-editor/

"United Airlines and *Rhapsody in Blue*"

BY RYAN RAUL BAÑAGALE

"Ryan's blog post is a microcosm of his book *Arranging Gershwin,* which explores ways in which arrangements of George Gershwin's *Rhapsody in Blue* define and redefine nationalist associations, taking it from a New York soundscape to an American icon to a corporate logo to an international anthem. Like most of my favorite posts on the OUPblog, Ryan discusses a work familiar to many and points out aspects you might not have noticed, broadening your interpretation and enriching your experience of the work."

—ANNA-LISE SANTELLA, Senior Editor, Music Reference, Oxford University Press

---

As anyone who has flown United in the past quarter-century knows, the company has a long-standing history with George Gershwin's *Rhapsody in Blue.* The piece appears in its television advertisements, its airport terminals, and even its preflight announcements. However, the history of United's use of the piece is far from straightforward. This brand-new safety video offers a compelling case in point.

Like recent videos by Air New Zealand and Delta Airlines, United's safety briefing is designed to keep our attention as it reiterates the standard safety announcements that we know all too well. The video rewards paying close attention on multiple viewings. In fact, there are several airline-travel and United-specific "Easter Eggs." A few of my favorites appear in the Las Vegas section. A tour bus traversing the Las Vegas Strip scrolls "lavatory occupied" and later "baggage on carousel 2." Perhaps more subtle is a movie poster for a film titled "Elbow Room 2." Look closely and you will see that it features a shot encountered later in the safety video as a James Bond–looking figure goes hand to hand against his nemesis a cable car—a clear reference to the 1979 film *Moonraker* for the alert viewer.

Under the banner "Safety is Global," the familiar themes of the *Rhapsody* are musically arranged while diverse members of the United flight crew provide instructions from a series of specific and generic international locales. Certainly, the visuals play a key role in signaling our recognition of these surroundings: the Eiffel Tower and street corner cafe for Paris, a pagoda in front of Mt. Fuji for Japan, casinos and neon signs for Las Vegas, snow-covered peaks and a ski gondola for the Alps, kangaroos for Australia, a Vespa scooter and Mt. Edna for Italy, Chilean flamingos for the bird sanctuary, and palm trees and white-sands for the tropical beach.

But perhaps most important in drawing out the setting of each scene are the dramatic—if not clichéd—musical arrangements of *Rhapsody in Blue.* While in France a pair of accordions play the introductory bars of the piece while a pilot welcomes us aboard and reminds us to heed their instruction. A flight attendant hops a cab to Newark Airport (United's East Coast hub) to the strains of a jazz combo setting of the love theme. A tenor saxophone improvises lightly around this most famous melody of the *Rhapsody* while she provides instruction on how to use the seatbelt from the bumpy backseat. A gong signals a move to Asia, where we encounter the ritornello theme of the *Rhapsody* on a plucked zither and bamboo flute. The bright lights of the Las Vegas strip (where we learn about power outages) and a James Bond–inspired depiction of the Swiss Alps (where we learn about supplemental oxygen) are accompanied by the traditional symphonic arrangement of the *Rhapsody* created by Ferde Grofé. Curious kangaroos learn about life vests as the ritornello theme is heard on a harmonica punctuated by a didgeridoo and a rain stick. A mandolin plucks out the shuffle theme while a flight attendant extinguishes a volcano like a birthday candle—no smoking allowed! Finally, steel drums transport us to a Caribbean bird sanctuary, and a tenor saxophone playing the stride theme to a laid-back, quasi-bossa nova groove relocates us to the beach.

Although each of these settings is somewhat stereotypical in its sonic and visual depiction of its respective locale, such treatment of the *Rhapsody* stands as less formulaic than past attempts at international representation by the airline. Both domestic and international advertisements have adapted the *Rhapsody*.

Although the video is a bit rough, by comparison to "Safety is Global," the visuals and instrumentation choices are much more stereotypical. We clearly hear the "orientalist" signifiers at play: a *taiko* drum, a *shakuhachi* flute, a trio of *pipas*. But just as this commercial provides its American market with a glimpse at Asian cultures through the streamlined gaze of corporate advertising, a commercial aired in Japan in 1994 provides an equally reductive depiction of the United States.

The spot features a Japanese puppet of the traditional Bunraku style seated on an airplane as the voiceover announces a series of locales that travelers could visit at ever-increasing award levels. The puppet appears in a succession of wardrobes representative of each destination with arrangements of *Rhapsody in Blue* emphasizing each costume change: a shamisen accompanies the traditional Japanese kimono, an erhu for the silk Chinese robe, a Hawaiian slide guitar for a bright floral patterned shirt and yellow lei, a fiddle-driven two-step for a cowboy hat and bolo tie, and finally a calypso, steel drum for the white Italian sports coat and dark sunglasses—a clear reference to Don Johnson and *Miami Vice*. The commercial not only effectively promotes United's frequent flyer program but also reinforces its corporate logos—both motto and music—to an international market. Through easily identifiable visual and sonic representations of destinations in the United States from Hawaii to Texas to Florida, it also promotes a positive—if not stereotypical—view of American culture using one of its most recognizable musical works.

And this is ultimately what the "Safety is Global" video accomplishes as well. By treating *Rhapsody in Blue* to a variety of musical arrangements, United Airlines has re-staked its claim on the *Rhapsody* not as its corporate theme music, but also as an international anthem. Its visualization of the *Rhapsody* over the course of time repositions the piece from a uniquely American (or specifically New Yorker) theme to one that aims to unite us all through the friendly skies.

RYAN RAUL BAÑAGALE is Assistant Professor of Music at Colorado College. He is author of *Arranging Gershwin: Rhapsody in Blue and the Creation of an American Icon*.

Originally published on 28 August 2014 at http://blog.oup.com/2014/08/united-airlines-gershwin-rhapsody-blue/

"Why study paradoxes?"

BY ROY T. COOK

"My favourite thing about the OUPblog is the diversity of the content we publish. Working on the blog every day means I get to read about fascinating subjects I know very little about. For example, articles like 'Why study paradoxes?' by Roy T. Cook introduced me to the concept of mathematical paradoxes. Mathematics was far from my favourite subject in school, but this article makes a very complex mathematical concept easy to understand as well as engaging and entertaining. In fact, this article captivated me to such an extent that I researched other mathematical paradoxes when I went home after work. Something I never thought I'd do!"

—**DANIEL PARKER,** OUPblog Deputy Editor (2014–present)

Why should you study paradoxes? The easiest way to answer this question is with a story.

In 2002 I was attending a conference on self-reference in Copenhagen, Denmark. During one of the breaks I got a chance to chat with Raymond Smullyan, who is, amongst other things, an accomplished magician, a distinguished mathematical logician, and perhaps the most well-known popularizer of "Knight and Knave" (K&K) puzzles.

K&K puzzles involve an imaginary island populated by two tribes: the Knights and the Knaves. Knights always tell the truth, and Knaves always lie (further, members of both tribes are forbidden to engage in activities that might lead to paradoxes or situations that break these rules). Other than their linguistic behavior, there is nothing that distinguishes Knights from Knaves.

Typically, K&K puzzles involve trying to answer questions based on assertions made by, or questions answered by, an inhabitant of the island. For example, a classic K&K puzzle involves meeting an islander at a fork in the road, where one path leads to riches and success and the other leads to pain and ruin. You are allowed to ask the islander one question, after which you must pick a path. Not knowing to which tribe the islander belongs, and hence whether she will lie or tell the truth, what question should you ask?

(Answer: You should ask, "Which path would someone from the other tribe say was the one leading to riches and success?" and then take the path not indicated by the islander.)

Back to Copenhagen in 2002: Seizing my chance, I challenged Smullyan with the following K&K puzzle, of my own devising:

There is a nightclub on the island of Knights and Knaves known as the Prime Club. The Prime Club has one strict rule: the number of occupants in the club must be a prime number at all times.

The Prime Club also has strict bouncers (who stand outside the doors and do not count as occupants) enforcing this rule. In addition, a strange tradition has become customary at the Prime Club: every so often the occupants form a conga line, and sing a song. The first lyric of the song is:

"At least one of us in the club is a Knave."

and is sung by the first person in the line. The second lyric of the song is:

"At least two of us in the club are Knaves."

and is sung by the second person in the line. The third person (if there is one) sings:

"At least three of us in the club are Knaves."

And so on down the line, until everyone has sung a verse.

One day you walk by the club, and hear the song being sung. How many people are in the club?

Smullyan's immediate response to this puzzle was something like "That can't be solved—there isn't enough information." But he then stood alone in the corner of the reception area for about five minutes, thinking, before returning to confidently (and correctly, of course) answer "Two!"

I won't spoil things by giving away the solution—I'll leave that mystery for interested readers to solve on their own. (Hint: if the song is sung with any other prime number of islanders in the club, a paradox results!) I will note that the song is equivalent to a more formal construction involving a list of sentences of the form:

At least one of sentences S1 – Sn is false.
At least two of sentences S1 – Sn is false.
⋮ ⋮ ⋮ ⋮ ⋮ ⋮ ⋮ ⋮ ⋮
At least *n* of sentences S1 – Sn is false.

The point of this story isn't to brag about having stumped a famous logician (even for a mere five minutes), although I admit that this episode (not only stumping Smullyan, but meeting him in the first place) is still one of the highlights of my academic career.

Instead, the story, and the puzzle at the center of it, illustrates the reasons why I find paradoxes so fascinating and worthy of serious intellectual effort. The standard story regarding why paradoxes are so important is that, although they are sometimes silly in and of themselves, paradoxes indicate that there is something deeply flawed in our understanding of some basic philosophical notion (truth, in the case of the semantic paradoxes linked to K&K puzzles).

Another reason for their popularity is that they are a lot of fun. Both of these are really good reasons for thinking deeply about paradoxes. But neither is the real reason why I find them so fascinating. The real reason I find paradoxes so captivating is that they are much more mathematically complicated, and as a result much more mathematically interesting, than standard accounts (which typically equate paradoxes with the presence of some sort of circularity) might have you believe.

The Prime Club puzzle demonstrates that whether a particular collection of sentences is or is not paradoxical can depend on all sorts of surprising mathematical properties, such as whether there is an even or odd number of sentences in the collection, or whether the number of sentences in the collection is prime or composite, or all sorts of even weirder and more surprising conditions.

Other examples demonstrate that whether a construction (or, equivalently, a K&K story) is paradoxical can depend on whether the referential relation involved in the construction (i.e., the relation that holds between two sentences if one refers to the other) is symmetric, or is transitive.

The paradoxicality of still another type of construction, involving infinitely many sentences, depends on whether cofinitely many of the sentences each refer to cofinitely many of the other sentences in the construction (a set is cofinite if its complement is finite). And this only scratches the surface!

The more I think about and work on paradoxes, the more I marvel at how complicated the mathematical conditions for generating paradoxes are: it takes a lot more than the mere presence of circularity to generate a mathematical or semantic paradox, and stating exactly what is minimally required is still too difficult a question to answer precisely. And that's why I work on paradoxes: their surprising mathematical complexity and mathematical beauty. Fortunately for me, there is still a lot of work that remains to be done, and a lot of complexity and beauty remaining to be discovered.

ROY T. COOK is Professor of Philosophy at the University of Minnesota–Twin Cities, a research fellow of the Minnesota Center for Philosophy of Science, and an associate fellow of the Northern Institute of Philosophy at the University of Aberdeen. He owns approximately 2.5 million LEGO bricks, teaches courses on comics, and has cats named Freckles and Mr. Prickely. He is also the author of *The Yablo Paradox: An Essay on Circularity*.

Originally published on 7 September 2014 at http://blog.oup.com/2014/09/why-study-paradoxes/

"Scots wha play: An English Shakespikedian Scottish independence referendum mashup"

BY ROBERT CRAWFORD

"Shakespeare's plays have been endlessly adapted. When done well, these adaptations can be wonderful, but rewriting and re-interpreting Shakespeare is no simple feat. Robert Crawford so brilliantly dramatized the Scottish referendum and set it against the backdrop of arguably one of the most important works of literature that takes place in Scotland, *Macbeth*. It's undeniably comedic, but there is also something somber about dramatizing one of the most important events in recent British history and relating it to a classic tale of power, ambition, and corruption."

—**JULIA CALLAWAY**, OUPblog Deputy Editor (2013–2015)

THE DATE: *18 September 2014, Fateful Day of Scotland's Independence Referendum*

THE PLACE: *A Sceptred Isle*

DRAMATIS PERSONAE:
Alexander the Great, First Minister of Scotland
Daveheart, Prime Minister of the Britons
Assorted Other Ministers, Attendant Lords, Lordlings, Politicos, and Camp Followers
Three Witches

A Botnet of Midges
The Internet (A Sprite)
A Helicopter
Dame Scotia
St. George of Osborne
Boris de Balliol, Mayor of Londres
UKIP (An Acronym)
Chorus

ACT I: *A Blasted Heath.*

Enter THREE WITCHES

When shall we three meet again,
In thunder, lightning, or in rain?

When the referendum's done,
When the battle's lost and won.

That will be when Salmond's gone.

Where the place?

Hampstead Heath.

Better Together unto death!

Is that your phone?

Daveheart calls: anon! —

Fair is foul, and foul is fair:
Hover through the plebs and filthy air.

[*WITCHES vanish.*]

ACT II: *The Scottish Camp (Voters at Dawn)*

Enter a SMALL FOLKS' CHORUS, Botnet Midges,
Who flap their wings, and then commence this chant:

See here assembled in the Scottish Camp
The Thane of Yes, Lord Naw-Naw, Doctor Spin.
Old folk forget; yet all shall be forgot,
But we'll remember, with advantages,
This Referendum Day. Then shall that name
And date, familiar as our household words—
Alex the Great, the eighteenth of September—
And many, many here who cast their votes,
A true sorority, a band of brothers,
Long be remembered—long as "Auld Lang Syne"—
For she or he who votes along with me
Shall be my sibling; be they curt or harsh
This day shall gentle their condition:
Scots students down in England now a-bed
Shall think themselves accursed, they were not here,
Casting their votes in this our referendum.

ACT III: *On Arthur's Seat, a Mount Olympus*
Near the Scots' Parliament at Holyrood

Proud Edward Milibrand, Daveheart, Nicholas Clegg,
And Anthony a Blair perch on the crags
With English Exiles. Now Lord Devomax speaks:

Stands England where it did? Alas, poor country,
Almost afraid to know itself, a stateless
Nation, post-imperial, undevolved;
Still sadly lacking its own Parliament,
It commandeers to deal with its affairs
The British Parliament, whose time it wastes
With talk of what pertains to England only,
And so abuses that quaint institution
As if it were its own, not for these islands
Set in a silver sea from Sark to Shetland.

[Exit, pursued by A. BLAIR]

ACT IV: *The Archipelago (High Noon)*

Enter THE INTERNET, A Sprite, who sings:

Full fathom five Westminster lies;
Democracy begins to fade;
Stout, undevolved, John Bull still eyes
Imperial power so long mislaid;
England must suffer a sea-change
Into something small and strange,
MPs hourly clang Big Ben:

DING-DONG!

Come, John Bull, and toll Big Ben.

ACT V: *South London: top floor of the Shard*

Boris de Balliol, St. George of Osborne,
Attendant Lords, and Chorus Bankerorum,
Et Nympharum Tamesis et Parliamentorum

Sheet lightnings flash offstage while clashing cymbals
Crescendo in a thunderous night's farrage.

ST GEORGE: Blow, winds, and crack your cheeks! Rage! Blow!
Ye exit polls and hurricanoes spout!
Come, Boris, here's the place. Stand still.

How fearful

And dizzy 'tis, to cast one's eyes so low!
The crows and choughs, that wing the midway air
Seem gross as bankers' apps: here from this Shard
See floors of smug short-sellers, dreadful traders
Inside a giant gherkin, and the City
Fraternity of *inegalité*
Spread out around us while its denizens
Appear like lice.

ATTENDANT LORDS: Scotia and Boris, hail!

BORIS: O Bella, Bella Caledonia,

Hic Boris Maior, Londinii Imperator,
Ego—

Fanfare of hautboys, bagpipes, and a tucket.

ST. GEORGE: A tucket!

BORIS: Tempus fugit.

CHORUS: Fuckaduckit!

Pipers, desist! Your music from this height
Has calmed the storm, and, blithely, while we wait
For the result to come from Holyrood,
So charms the ear that, clad in English tartans—
The Hunting Cholmondesley, the Royal Agincourt,
And chic crisscrosses of the National Trust—
Our city here, ravished by this fair sound
Of tweeted pibroch, YouTubed from the Shard
To Wapping, Westminster, and Heathrow's tarmac,
While gazing up from bingo and Big Macs,
Brooding upon our disunited kingdom,
Stands all agog to hear Dame Scotia speak.

Scotia descends, ex machina helecopteris

HELICOPTER: Bzzzzzzzzzzzzzzzzzzzzzzzzzzzz.

SCOTIA: O England, England, your tight cabinet's
Sly Oxbridge public-schoolboy millionaires
Fight while your country sinks beneath their yoke;

It weeps, it bleeds; and each new day a gash
Is added to those wounds: new Europhiles
Repulsed, the world repelled; England whose riots
Failed to stop students' fees for your own folk
Or to contain their escalating cost.
Sad, catastrophic, calculating drones
Miscalculating loans, kicking the arts,
England betrayed by Scoto-Anglish Blair
Into wrong wars and then to Gordon Brown,
Jowled lord of loss and light-touch regulation.
O England, England! Rise and be a nation
United under your own Parliament!
Methinks I am a prophet now inspired
And thus, inspiring, do foretell of you:
Your Europhobia must not endure,
For violent fires must soon burn out themselves;
Small showers last long, but sudden storms are short.
Learn from the Scots: plant windfarms, make yourself
A Saudi Arabia of tidal power,
Though not of gender; learn, too, from the French,
There is no need to stay a sceptred isle,
Scuffed other Eden, demi-paradise;
No fortress, built by UKIP for themselves,
Against infection in their Brussels wars;
Be happy as a nation on an island
That's not England's alone, a little world,
This precious stone set in a silver sea,
Which serves to link it now with all the globe,
Or as the front door to a happy home,
Be, still, the envy of less happier lands,
And set up soon an English Parliament,

Maybe in London, Britain's other eye,
Maybe in Yorkshire, so you may become
A better friend to Scotland whose folk love
This blessed plot, this earth, and independence.

She zooms northwards.

ROBERT CRAWFORD's *Bannockburns: Scottish Independence and Literary Imagination, 1314–2014* was published by Edinburgh University Press in 2014. He is also the author of *Testament*, a collection of poems (certainly not containing the above, but including poems on the theme of Scottish independence). He teaches in the School of English at the University of St. Andrews.

Originally published on 17 September 2014 at: http://blog.oup.com/2014/09/scottish-independence-referendum-macbeth-shakespeare/

"The *Oxford DNB* at 10: New research opportunities in the humanities"

BY DAVID HILL RADCLIFFE

"One of the pleasures of the OUPblog is the space it offers for free thinking and for looking ahead. Here Professor David Hill Radcliffe of Virginia Tech University ponders the future for humanities research as large digital works—including the *Oxford Dictionary of National Biography*—are reconfigured to cast new light on the past. The potential to interconnect millions of people, events, and artefacts presents opportunities of which we're only now becoming aware."

—**PHILIP CARTER**, Publication Editor, *Oxford Dictionary of National Biography*, Oxford University Press

---

The publication of the *Oxford Dictionary of National Biography* in September 2004 was a milestone in the history of scholarship, not least for crossing from print to digital publication. Prior to this moment, a small army of biographers, myself among them, had worked almost entirely from paper sources, including the stately volumes of the first, Victorian "DNB" and its twentieth-century print supplement volumes. But the *Oxford DNB* (*ODNB*) of 2004 was conceived from the outset as a database and published online as web pages, not paper pages reproduced in facsimile. In doing away with the page image as a means of structuring digital information, the online *ODNB* made an important step which scholarly monographs and articles might do well to emulate.

Database design has seen dramatic changes since 2004—shifting from the relational model of columns and rows, to semi-structured data used with XML technologies, to the unstructured forms used for linking data across repositories. The implications of these developments for the future of the *ODNB* remain to be seen, but there is every reason to believe that its content will be increasingly accessed in ways other than the format of the traditional biographical essay. Essays are not going away, of course. But they will be supplemented by the arrays of tables, charts, maps, and graphs made possible by linked data. Indeed, the *ODNB* has been moving in this direction since 2004 with the addition of thousands of curated links between individuals (recorded in biographical essays) and the social hierarchies and networks to which they belonged (presented in thematic list and group entries)—and then on to content by or about a person held in archives, museums, or galleries worldwide.

Online the *ODNB* offers scholars the opportunity to select, group, and parse information not just at the level of the article, but also in more detailed ways—and this is where computational matters get interesting. I currently use the *ODNB* online as a resource for a digital prosopography attached to a collection of documents called "Lord Byron and his Times," tracking relationships among more than 12,000 Byron contemporaries mentioned in nineteenth-century letters and memoirs; of these people a remarkable 5,000 have entries in the *ODNB*. The traditional object of prosopography was to collect small amounts of information about large numbers of persons, using patterns to draw inferences about slenderly documented lives. But when computation is involved, a prosopography can be used with linked data to parse large amounts of information about large numbers of persons. As a result, one can attend to particularities, treating individuals as members of a group or social network without reducing them to the uniformity of a class identity. Digital prosopography thus returns us to something like the nineteenth-century liberalism that inspired Sir Leslie Stephen's original *DNB* (1885–1900).

The key to finding patterns in large collections of lives and documents, the evolution of technology suggests, is to atomize the data. As a writer of biographies I would select from documentary sources, collecting the facts of a life and translating them into the form of an *ODNB* essay. Creating a record in a prosopography involves a similar kind of abstraction: working from (say) an *ODNB* entry, I abstract facts from the prose, encoding names and titles and dates in a semi-structured XML template that can then be used to query my archive, comprising data from previous *ODNB* abstractions and other sources. For instance: "find relationships among persons who corresponded with Byron (or Harrow School classmates, or persons born in Nottinghamshire, etc.) mentioned in the *Quarterly Review*." An XML prosopography is but a step towards recasting the information as flexible, concise, and extensible semantic data.

While human readers can easily distinguish the character-string "Oxford" as referring to the place, the university, or the press, this is a challenge for computation—like distinguishing "Byron" the poet from "Byron" the admiral. One can attack this problem by using algorithms to compare adjacent strings, or one can encode strings by hand to disambiguate them, or use a combination of both. Digital *ODNB* essays are good candidates for semantic analysis since their structure is predictable and they are dense with significant names of persons, places, events, and relationships that can be used for data-linking. One translates character-strings into semantic references, groups the references into relationships, and expresses the relationships in machine-readable form.

A popular model for parsing semantic data is via "triples": statements in the form subject / property / object, which describe a relationship between the subject and the object: the tree / is in / the quad. It is powerful because it can describe anything, and its statements can be yoked together to create new statements. For example: "Lord Byron wrote *Childe Harold*" and "John Murray published *Childe Harold*" are both triples. Once the three components are translated into semantically disambiguated machine-readable URIs (Uniquely Referring Identifiers), computation can infer that "John Murray published Lord Byron."

Now imagine the contents of the *ODNB* expressed not as 60,000 biographical essays but as several billion such statements. In fact, this is far from unthinkable, given the nature of the material and progress being made in information technology. The result is a wonderful back-to-the-future moment with Leslie Stephen's Victorian *DNB* wedded to Charles Babbage's calculating machine: the simplicity of the triple and the power of finding relations embedded within them. Will the fantasies of positivist historians finally be realized? Not likely; while computation is good at questions of "who," "what," "where," and "when," it is not so good at "why" and "how." Biographers and historians are unlikely to find themselves out of a job anytime soon. On the contrary, once works like the *ODNB* are rendered machine-readable and cross-query-able, scholars will find more work on their hands than they know what to do with.

So the publication of the *ODNB* online in September 2004 will be fondly remembered as a liminal moment when humanities scholarship crossed from paper to digital. The labour of centuries of research was carried across that important threshold, recast in a medium enabling new kinds of investigation the likes of which—ten years on—we are only beginning to contemplate.

Professor DAVID HILL RADCLIFFE is a literary historian and antiquary in the Department of English at Virginia Tech. His current study is of the social and literary networks involving British romantic writers connected with Byron, the basis for the database "Lord Byron and his Times."

Originally published on 18 September 2014 at http://blog.oup.com/2014/09/oxford-dnb-at-10-online/

"Facebook, the gender binary, and third-person pronouns"

BY LAL ZIMMAN

"Gender and sexual identity have been powerful catalysts for change in the English lexicon in recent decades. In this post, Lal Zillman explores how new ways of thinking about gender are challenging one of the most fundamental parts of the English vocabulary: pronouns."

—KATHERINE MARTIN, Head of US Dictionaries, Oxford University Press

---

The death rattle of the gender binary has been ringing for decades now, leaving us to wonder when it will take its last gasp. In this third decade of third-wave feminism and the queer critique, dismantling the binary remains a critical task in the gender revolution. Language is among the most socially pervasive tools through which culture is negotiated, but in a language like English, with its minimal linguistic marking of gender, it can be difficult to find concrete signs that linguistic structures are changing to reflect new ways of thinking about the gender binary rather than simply repackaging old ideas.

One direction we might look, though, is toward the gendering of third-person pronouns, which is what led me to write this post about pronouns on Facebook. Yes, Facebook. The social media giant may not be your first thought when it comes to feminist language activism, but this year's shift in the way Facebook categorizes gender is among the most widely felt signs of a sea change in institutional attitudes about gendered third-person pronouns. Although Facebook does not have the same force as the educational system, governments, or traditional print media, it carries its own linguistic cachet established through its corporate authority, its place in the cultural negotiation of coolness and social connection, and its near-inescapable presence in everyday life.

In response to long-standing calls from transgender and gender-nonconforming users to broaden its approach to gender, Facebook announced earlier this year that it would offer a new set of options. Rather than limiting members of the site to the selection of female or male, an extensive list of gender identities is offered, along with the option of a custom entry, including labels like *agender, bigender, gender fluid, gender-nonconforming, trans person, two-spirit, transgender (wo)man*, and *cisgender (i.e. nontransgender) (wo)man.*

With all of the potential complexity afforded by these categories, Facebook couldn't rely on a simple algorithm of assigning gendered pronouns for those occasions on which the website generates a third person reference to the user (e.g. "Wish ___ a happy birthday!"). Instead, it asks which set of pronouns a user prefers among three options: *he/him/his*, *she/her/hers*, or *they/them/theirs*. As a result, there are two important ways that Facebook's reconsideration of its gender classification system goes beyond the listing of additional gender categories. The first is the more obvious of the two: offering singular *they* as an option for those who prefer gender-neutral reference forms. The other is simply the practice of asking for a pronoun preference rather than deriving it from gender or sex.

Sanctioning the use of singular *they* as a gender-neutral pronoun counters the centuries-old grammarian's complaint that they can only be used in reference to plural third-person referents. Proponents of singular *they*, however, point out that the pronoun has been used by some of the English-speaking world's finest writers and that it was in widespread use even before blatantly misogynistic language policies determined that *he* should be the gender-neutral pronoun in official texts of the British government. More recently, an additional source of support for singular *they* has arisen: for those who do not wish to be slotted into one side of the gender binary or the other, *they* is perhaps the most intuitive way to avoid gendered third-person pronouns because of its already familiar presence in most dialects of English. (Other options include innovative pronouns like *ze/hir/hirs* or *ey/em/em's*.) In this case, a speaker must choose between upholding grammatical conventions and affirming someone's identity.

But wait, you might ask—don't we need a distinction between singular and plural *they*? How are we supposed to know when someone is talking about a single person and when they're talking about a group? Though my post isn't necessarily meant to defend the use of singular *they* in reference to specific individuals (an argument others have made quite extensively), this point is worth addressing briefly if only to dispel the notion that the standard pronoun system is logical while deviations are somehow logically flawed. As the pronoun charts included here illustrate, there is already a major gap in the standard English pronoun system when compared to many other languages: a distinction between singular and plural *you*. Somehow we get by, however, relying on context and sometimes asking for clarification. Could we do the same with *they*?

The second pronoun-related change Facebook has made—asking for preferred pronouns rather than determining them based on gender category—is a more fundamental challenge to the normative take on assigning pronouns. According to conventional wisdom, a speaker will select whether to use *she* or *he* based on certain types of information about the person being referred to: how their bodily sex is perceived, how they present their gender, and in some cases other contextual factors like their name. To be uncertain about which gendered pronoun to use can be a source of great anxiety, exemplified by cultural artifacts like *Saturday Night Live's* androgynous character from the 1990s known only as Pat. No one ever asks Pat about their gender because to do so would presumably be a grave insult, as Pat apparently has no idea that they have an androgynous appearance (were you able to follow me, despite the singular *they*'s?).

But transgender and queer communities are increasingly turning this logic on its head. Rather than risk being "mis-pronouned," as community members sometimes call it, it is becoming the norm for introductions in many trans and queer contexts to include pronouns preferences along with names. For instance, my name is Lal and I prefer *he/him/his* pronouns. (Even the custom of calling these "male" pronouns has been critiqued on the basis that one needn't identify as male in order to prefer *he/him/his* pronouns.) The goal behind this move is to remove the tension of uncertainty and to avoid potential offense or embarrassment before it takes place. But this is not just a practice for transgender and gender-nonconforming people; the ideal is that no one's pronoun preferences be taken for granted. Instead of determining pronouns according to appearance, *they* become a matter of open negotiation in which one can demonstrate an interest in using language that feels maximally respectful to others.

Facebook's adoption of this new approach to pronouns, despite prescriptive grammarians' objections, suggests that the acceptance and use of singular *they* is expanding. More than that, it furthers the normalization of self-selected pronouns since even those who are totally unfamiliar with the use of singular *they* as a preferred pronoun, or the very idea of pronoun preferences, may be faced with unexpected pronouns in their daily newsfeeds.

For those of us at academic institutions with sizable transgender and gender-nonconforming communities, the practices discussed here may already be under way on campus. During my time teaching at Reed College, for instance, I found students to be enthusiastic about including pronoun preferences in our beginning-of-semester introductions even in classes where everyone's pronoun preferences aligned with normative expectations.

My goal here isn't to argue that the gender binary is dissolving in the face of new pronoun practices. Indeed, linguistic negotiations of gender and sexual binaries are far too complex to draw such a simple conclusion. However, what I do want to suggest is that we are in the midst of some kind of shift in the way pronouns are used and understood among speakers of English. Describing a more fully complete change of this sort, linguistic anthropologist Michael Silverstein has explained how religious and political ideology among speakers of Early Modern English resulted in a collapse of the second-person pronouns *thou* (singular, informal) and *you* (plural, formal). In the present case, rapidly changing ideologies about the gender binary may be pushing us toward a different organization of third-person pronouns.

The effect of Facebook on linguistic practice more broadly has yet to be fully uncovered, but its capital-driven flexibility and omnipresence in contemporary social life suggests that it may be a powerful tool in ideologically driven language change.

LAL ZIMMAN is the co-editor of *Queer Excursions: Retheorizing Binaries in Language, Gender, and Sexuality* with Jenny Davis and Joshua Raclaw and a Visiting Assistant Professor at Reed College. His research, which brings together ethnographic, sociophonetic, and discourse analytic frameworks, deals with the relationship between gender, sexuality, and embodiment in the linguistic practices of transgender and LGBQ communities.

Originally published on 23 September 2014 at: http://blog.oup.com/2014/09/facebook-gender-binary-third-person-pronouns/

"In defence of horror"

BY DARRYL JONES

"This post by Professor Darryl Jones is, I think, an excellent example of what a blog post is capable of doing. It's intelligently written and draws insightful parallels between the gory horror films we have watched at home or in the cinema and classical literature, where there is more gore than could potentially be shown on celluloid. *Cannibal Holocaust* may shock with its graphic scenes, but Euripides had a mother parading about with her son's head on a stick thousands of years before. Professor Jones's post is also entertaining, showing that the blog is an ideal forum for the most academic ideas to be conveyed in an engaging manner. It's one of my favourite blog posts for all of these reasons."

—**KIRSTY DOOLE,** OUPblog Deputy Editor (2010–2014) and Publicity Manager, Oxford University Press

---

A human eyeball shoots out of its socket, and rolls into a gutter. A child returns from the dead and tears the beating heart from his tormentor's chest. A young man has horrifying visions of his mother's decomposing corpse. A baby is ripped from its living mother's womb. A mother tears her son to pieces, and parades around with his head on a stick . . . These are scenes from the notorious, banned "video nasty" films *Eaten Alive*, *Zombie Flesh Eaters*, *I Spit on Your Grave*, *Anthropophagous: The Beast*, and *Cannibal Holocaust*.

Well, no. They could be—but they're not. All these scenes and images can be found safely inside the respectable covers of Oxford World's Classics, in the works of Edgar Allan Poe, M.R. James, James Joyce, William Shakespeare, and Euripides. Only the first two of these are avowedly writers of horror, and none of these books comes with any kind of public health warning or age-suitability guideline. What does this mean?

Euripides's *The Bacchae*, first performed around 400 BC, is one of the foundational works of the Western literary canon. In describing graphically the actions of Agave and her Maenads, dismembering King Pentheus and putting his head on a pole, it also sets the bar very high for artistic representations of violence and gore. The episode of the baby ripped from the mother's womb to which I alluded in the first paragraph is from *Macbeth*, of course—it's Macduff's account of his own birth. And *Macbeth*, though certainly no slouch in the mayhem department, isn't even Shakespeare's most violent play. That would be *Titus Andronicus*, whose opening scene makes the connections between civilization and horror very clear, as Tamora, Queen of the Goths, sees her son brutally killed by the conquering Romans:

> See, lord and father, how we have performed
> Our Roman rites: Alarbus' limbs are lopp'd,
> And entrails feed the sacrificing fire,
> Whose smoke, like incense, doth perfume the sky.

What follows is well known: further mutilation, rape, cannibalism. Shocking, yes; surprising, no. After all, the greater part of the Western literary tradition follows, or celebrates, a faith whose own sacrificial rites have at their heart symbolic representations of torture and cannibalism, the cross and the host. A case could plausibly be made that the Western literary tradition is a tradition of horror. This may be an overstatement, but it's an argument with which any honest thinker has to engage.

The classic argument adduced in defence of the brutality of tragedy (a form which I have come to think of as highbrow horror) is the Aristotelian concept of *catharsis*, according to which the act of witnessing artistic representations of cruelty and monstrosity, pity and fear, purges the audience of these emotions, leaving them psychologically healthier. *Horror is good for you!* I confess I have always had difficulty accepting this hypothesis (though I recognize that many people far more learned and brilliant than I have had no trouble accepting it). It seems to be a classic example of an intellectual's gambit, a theory offered without recourse to any evidence. And yet catharsis is far preferable to another, more common, response to horror: the urge to censor or ban extreme documents and images in the name of public morality. If catharsis is Aristotelian, then this hypothesis is Pavlovian: horror conditions our responses; a tendency to watch violent acts leads inexorably to a tendency to commit violent acts. For many people, this seems to make intuitive sense (on more than one occasion, I've noticed people backing away from me when I tell them I work on horror), and it's the impetus behind the framing of the Video Recordings Act of 1984, after which *Cannibal Holocaust* and all those other video nasties were banned. As a number of commentators and critics have noted, there's no evidence for this Pavlovian hypothesis, either. Worse than that, there's a distinct class animus behind such thinking. You and I, cultured, literate, educated, middle-class folks that we are, are perfectly safe: when we watch *Cannibal Holocaust* (which I do, even if you don't) we know what we are seeing, we can contextualize the film, interpret it, recognize it for what it is. The problem, the argument implicitly goes, is not us, it is *them*, those festering, semi-bestial proletarians whose extant propensity for violence (always simmering beneath the surface) can only be stoked by watching these films. That's why no one seriously considers banning *The Bacchae* or *Titus Andronicus*—why any suggestion that we do so would be treated as an act of appalling philistinism. They are horror for the educated classes.

Horror is, unquestionably, an extreme art form. Like all avant-garde art, I would suggest, its real purpose is to force its audiences to confront the limits of their own tolerance—including, emphatically, their own tolerance for what is or is not art. Commonly, when hitting these limits, we respond with fear, frustration, and even rage. Even today, this is not an unusual reaction on first reading *Finnegans Wake*, for example: I see it occasionally in my students, who are (a) voluntarily students of literature, and (b) usually Irish, not to say actual Dubliners. So we shouldn't be surprised that audiences respond to horror with—well, with horror. But we need to recognize that the reasons for doing this are complex, and are deeply bound up with the meaning and function of art, and of civilization.

DARRYL JONES has taught at Trinity College Dublin since 1994. Prior to this he taught in the University of Lodz, Poland. He has held Visiting Professorships at Dartmouth College, New Hampshire; Babes Bolyai University, Cluj-Napoca, Romania; and Tongji University, Shanghai. He is the author or editor of nine books, including *Horror Stories: Classic Tales from Hoffmann to Hodgson, Horror: A Thematic History in Fiction and Film*, *It Came From the 1950s!: Popular Culture, Popular Anxieties* (with Elizabeth McCarthy and Bernice M. Murphy), and *M. R. James, Collected Ghost Stories.*

Originally published on 22 October 2014 at: http://blog.oup.com/2014/10/classic-horror-stories/

"Race relations in America and the case of Ferguson"

BY ARNE L. KALLEBERG

"How did a tragedy in a nondescript suburb of St. Louis, Missouri, bring race relations to the fore of American consciousness? In an interview with Arne L. Kalleberg, editor of *Social Forces*, Wayne Santoro and Lisa Broidy develop a framework for understanding the shooting that shook a nation, blending statistical objectivity with human nuance. Memorializing Michael Brown, they examine the intersection of policymakers, protesters, and public, uncovering not only a local but nationwide pattern of structural violence that makes 'Ferguson more typical than atypical.'"

—SONIA TSURUOKA,
OUPblog Deputy Editor (2015–present)

The fatal shooting of African American teenager Michael Brown, in Ferguson, Missouri, during a police altercation in August 2014, resulted in massive civil unrest and protests that received considerable attention from the United States and abroad. To gain further perspective on the situation in Ferguson and its implications for race relations in America, I spoke with Wayne A. Santoro and Lisa Broidy, authors of the article "Gendered Rioting: A General Strain Theoretical Approach" published in *Social Forces*.

Why do you think there has been so much media attention on the situation in Ferguson following the Michael Brown shooting?

Police shootings and the mistreatment of black citizens are not, unfortunately, uncommon in the United States. Protests like street marches have become so routinized that at best they get covered in the back pages of the local newspaper. But what no one can ignore are protests that turn violent. Whether we call them riots or rebellions, they are front-page news. They are dramatic and unpredictable, threaten life and property, and capture the media's attention. Policymakers cannot ignore them. After all, it is not every day that a state governor calls out the National Guard to maintain law and order. And whether the public views the protestors in a sympathetic or unsympathetic manner, we are mesmerized by the ongoing drama. How long will the rioting last? How will law enforcement respond? What will be the cost in lives lost and property destroyed?

Why do you think that the shooting of Michael Brown sparked protest by citizens? What was unique about the circumstances in Ferguson, or the Michael Brown case?

Four factors stand out, some unique to the incident and to Ferguson while others are more typical. First, the single best predictor of black riots is police shootings or abuse of blacks by police. Indeed, in our research we find that a particularly strong predictor of joining a riot is having experienced police mistreatment personally. Police harassment is the spark that ignites protests that turn violent. This was a central conclusion of the famous 1968 Kerner Commission, which studied black rioting in the late sixties.

Second, blacks in Ferguson have long complained about police harassment. Numerous blacks in Ferguson have recited to the media past experiences with police mistreatment. One resident recalled how he was roughed up by the police during a minor traffic stop. Another spoke of how she called the police for assistance only to have the police arrest her upon arrival. There was an incident in 2009 where a black man accused officers of beating him and then found out that he was subsequently charged with damaging government property by getting his blood on their police uniforms. Some of this mistreatment is suggested by data in Ferguson on race, traffic stops, and arrests.

Blacks comprise 67% of Ferguson's population (in 2010) but account for 86% of all traffic stops by the police and 93% of all arrests resulting from these stops. Blacks are also twice as likely as white drivers to have the police search their car despite the fact that whites are more likely to have contraband found in their car. These data point to racially biased police practices. This is not unique to Ferguson, and in fact national survey data tell us that it is common knowledge among blacks that the police often act as agents of repression. For instance, in a *New York Times*/CBS News national survey conducted ten days after the shooting, 45% of blacks reported that they had personally experienced police discrimination because of their race (7% of whites reported this experience). Similarly, 71% of blacks believed that local police were more likely to use deadly force against a black person (only 31% of whites agreed). Thus, it is a racially charged shooting of a black man within the context of widespread experiences of police racial abuse that fuels motivations for protest and the belief that the use of violence against the state is legitimate.

Third, the circumstances of the shooting matter. Was the shooting a legitimate or excessive use of police force? It is relevant that so many local blacks think that not only was Michael Brown unarmed (which is undisputed) but that he had his hands raised and was surrendering at the time of the shooting. What matters is not so much whether the "hands raised and surrendering" scenario is accurate (this likely will remain in dispute) but that so many local residents found it believable that a white police officer would shoot six times an unarmed black man trying to surrender. People believe narratives that resonate with their personal experiences, and this again tells us something about what these personal experiences with the police have been.

Fourth, blacks in Ferguson have been excluded almost completely from positions of power. People protest when their voices are not being heard, and in Ferguson it appears that those who make policy decisions and influence police behavior are particularly deaf to the concerns of the black community. Referring to an incident where Ferguson officials were unresponsive to a relatively minor request, one black resident remarked "You get tired. You keep asking, you keep asking. Nothing gets done." One arena where this exclusion is evident is in the police department. In the Ferguson police department only 3 (some report 4) of 53 commissioned officers—about 6%—are black. Recall that Ferguson is 67% black. Police departments are seldom responsive to minority communities when policy and street-level enforcement decisions are made solely by whites. Moreover, minority distrust of the police is likely when few police officers are minority. The racial power disparity is evident in elected positions as well. As Jeff Smith (2014) wrote in the *New York Times*, "Ferguson has a virtually all-white power structure: a white mayor; a school board with six white members and one Hispanic, which recently suspended a highly regarded young black superintendent who then resigned; a City Council with just one black member." Access to political positions and direct influence on policymaking tend to channel discontent into institutional arenas. Protest is a marker that a population is politically marginalized. Protest is inherently a response to blocked access and influence over the political system.

To what degree is Ferguson unique as opposed to being emblematic of race relations in America?

Ferguson is more typical than atypical. There remain in the United States deep and enduring racial disparities in socioeconomic status, wealth, and well-being. No other population in the United States has experienced the degree of residential segregation from whites as have blacks. We imprison black men at a staggering rate. What the Kerner Commission stated nearly 50 years ago remains true today: we are a "nation of two societies, one black, one white— separate and unequal." This inequality has been noted repeatedly by black residents in Ferguson, who see the local governing regime as unresponsive, the police force as hostile, and the school system as abysmal. Ferguson also is typical in that it reveals how views of racial progress and incidents like the shooting of Michael Brown are racially polarized. In the *New York Times*/CBS News survey noted above, 49% of blacks thought that the protests in Ferguson were about right or did not go far enough—only 19% of whites held such views.

In two ways, however, Ferguson seems atypical. First, in Ferguson, the growth in the black population relative to whites is a recent occurrence. In 1990, blacks comprised 25% of the city's population, but that percentage grew to 52% in 2000 and 67%

in 2010. This demographic transition was not followed by a corresponding transition in black access to political positions, the police force, union representation, and the like. Sociologists speak of the "backlash hypothesis," meaning that when whites feel threatened, such as by increases in the minority population, they respond with greater hostility to the "threatening" population. The recency of the demographic transition likely has altered the social and political dynamics of the city in ways that do not characterize other contemporary major cities in the United States, especially those that are majority black, like Detroit or Atlanta.

Second, Ferguson is unusual in the degree that the city uses the municipal court system and the revenue it generates as a way to raise city funds. Court fines make up the second-highest source of revenue for the city. This created a financial incentive to issue tickets and then impose excessive fees on people who did not pay. Data bear this out. Ferguson issued more than 1,500 warrants per 1,000 people in 2013, and this rate exceeds that of all other Missouri cities with a population larger than 10,000 people. To put this another way, Ferguson has a population of just over 21,000 people but issued more than 24,000 warrants, which adds up to three warrants per Ferguson household. Writes Frances Robles (2014) in the *New York Times*: "Young black men in Ferguson and surrounding cities routinely find themselves passed from jail to jail as they are picked up on warrants for unpaid fines." Thus, in Ferguson, the primary interactions between many black residents and the police take place because of these warrants. Recent work on social movements has argued that such daily insults and humiliations can play a strong role in motivating people to protest, and certainly serve to undermine trust in the local police and city policymakers.

What will be the likely short- and longer-term consequences of the Ferguson protests?

Understanding how policymakers and others respond to a protest—especially one that turns violent—is complex. There is no typical response, and historically one could cite examples of elites either trying to ameliorate the conditions that gave rise to the protest or responding in a more punitive manner. Nonetheless, in the short term, there are reasons to think that policymakers will respond in ways favorable to the local black community by addressing some of their grievances. As political scientist James Button has written, policymakers tend to respond more favorably to riots when riots are large enough to garner public and media attention but not so severe and widespread to cause major societal disruption. This describes the Ferguson riots, unlike, for instance, the riots during the late 1960s in the United States. Moreover, policymakers who are sympathetic to minorities tend to respond in ways more favorable to minorities than less receptive policymakers. Social movement scholars refer to this as a favorable "political opportunity structure." In the United States, the former tend to come from the ranks of the Democratic Party while the latter come from the ranks of the Republican Party. Thus, the fact that the Ferguson protests occurred during the Obama administration suggests a more ameliorative than punitive response, at least at the national level. It is not surprising that three times more blacks, 60% to 20%, report being satisfied rather than unsatisfied with how President Obama has responded to the situation in Ferguson.

There is some evidence that policymakers are indeed responding in ways favorable to the local black community and their grievances. For instance, Attorney General Eric H. Holder, Jr., announced an independent investigation of the shooting and traveled to Ferguson to meet with investigators. Moreover, his office has started a civil rights investigation into whether the police have repeatedly violated the civil rights of residents. At the local level, some changes also are evident. On 8 September 2014, the Ferguson City Council agreed to establish a citizen review board to monitor the local police department. The city also has pledged that it would revamp its policy of using court fines to fund such a large share of its city budget. For instance, the city council has eliminated a $50 warrant recall fee and a $15 notification fee.

It is more of a leap of faith, however, to expect major long-term changes in Ferguson because of the insurgency. There remains, for instance, an ongoing debate by scholars of the modern civil rights movement (*c.* 1955–1968) as to whether the more than decade-long movement produced meaningful change in the lives of most blacks. If a decade of protests produced less than satisfactory change in the opinion of some, what chance do the Ferguson protests have? In particular, there is little reason to think that levels of black poverty, unemployment, underemployment, and educational disparities will improve noticeably in Ferguson unless other social forces are brought into play. These more substantive changes are more likely to be produced by years of community organizing, securing elected positions, joining governing political coalitions with sympathetic allies, and favorable economic conditions like the growth of blue-collar employment opportunities.

Have white police shootings of minorities (or African Americans) become more or less common in recent years?

This is an empirical question and the relevant data are limited. There are no national data on police shootings that do not result in death. National data on police shootings that result in death come from three sources: the Federal Bureau of Investigation (FBI), the Bureau of Justice Statistics (BJS), and the Centers for Disease Control (CDC). However, data from each of these sources are limited. The FBI collects data on "justifiable homicide" by police as a voluntary component of the Supplemental Homicide Report data collected from police departments nationwide. Unfortunately few departments (less than 5%) voluntarily provide these data, leaving obvious questions about their representativeness and utility. Moreover, even if they were complete, these data would tell us little beyond the demographics of those killed. Particularly, we cannot discern the degree to which these incidents represent excessive use of force by police. BJS collects similar data on deaths that occur during an arrest. These data are collected at the state level and then reported to BJS. Compliance is better, with 48 states reporting. But it is not clear how complete or comparable the data from each state are.

Despite these shortcomings, there is one inescapable conclusion: blacks are disproportionately killed in police shootings. For instance, blacks comprise 13% of the US population but represent 32% of those killed by police between 2003 and 2009. The CDC compiles data from all death certificates nationwide, which includes data on "deaths by legal intervention." Using the online query system for firearm deaths by legal intervention from 1999–2011, the average rate at which blacks are killed is more than double that of whites (0.2/100,000 compared to 0.1/100,000).

Is there anything else you think we can learn about race relations or racially motivated social movements in the United States from the case of Ferguson?

A few lessons. First, we often talk about the civil rights movement in the past tense. We think of it as something that happened; we might even debate why it "ended" and what it accomplished. But Ferguson reminds us that the struggle for racial justice continues. It is not always so newsworthy, but every day many blacks and black advocacy organizations struggle to overcome racial barriers. Second, it underscores the deep racial divide in the United States. White and black views, especially concerning racial matters, are often polar opposite. Where whites see progress, blacks see setbacks. Where whites see black advancement, blacks see persistent racial disparities. Especially polarized are views on the criminal justice system and police. Third, there are costs to a society when a population is politically and economically marginalized. These costs may not always be apparent to outsiders nor make national headlines. But the price we pay for racial disparities is that violent protests will continue to be an enduring feature of the US landscape. The national memory of the Ferguson riots will fade only to be replaced by the next Ferguson-style protest. The question becomes what are we as individuals and as a collective willing to do to eradicate the racial inequality that motivates such protest?

ARNE L. KALLEBERG is the Kenan Distinguished Professor of Sociology at the University of North Carolina at Chapel

Hill and editor of *Social Forces*. WAYNE SANTORO, PhD, is a Professor of Sociology at the University of New Mexico. His work lies at the intersection of race, politics, and social movements. LISA BROIDY, PhD, is an Associate Professor of the School of Criminology and Criminal Justice at Griffith University. Santoro and Broidy are the authors of "Gendered Rioting: A General Strain Theoretical Approach," published in *Social Forces*.

Originally published on 26 October 2014 at: http://blog.oup.com/2014/10/race-relations-ferguson-michael-brown/

"The origin of work-hour regulations for house officers"

BY KENNETH M. LUDMERER

"The issue of work-hour regulations for house officers is the most contentious and emotional issue in medical education since the Flexner Report of 1910. The subject involves some timeless concerns in medical education—namely, the ultimate responsibility of medical education to the public, and the fact that cultural forces as well as scientific and professional developments shape the evolution of medical education and practice."

—**KENNETH M. LUDMERER,** OUPblog contributor and author of *Let Me Heal*

Interns and residents have always worked long hours in hospitals, and there has always been much to admire about this. Beyond the educational benefits that accrue from observing the natural history of disease and therapy, long hours help instill a sense of commitment to the patient. House officers learn that becoming a doctor means learning to meet the needs of others. This message has never been lost on them.

However, it has also long been recognized that house officers are routinely overworked. This point was emphasized in the first systematic study of graduate medical education, published in 1940. In the 1950s and 1960s, the hazards of sleep deprivation became known, including mood changes, depression, impaired cognition, diminished psychomotor functioning, difficulty with interpersonal relationships, and an increased risk of driving accidents. In the 1970s, the phenomenon of burnout was recognized. In the mid-1980s, after prospective payment of hospitals was introduced, the workload of house officers became greater still, as there were now many more patients to see, the patients were sicker, the level of care was more complex, and there was less time to care for patients. House officers understood they were in a dilemma where their high standards of professionalism were used by others to justify sometimes inhumane levels of work.

Despite their long hours, the public generally believed that house officers provided outstanding medical and surgical care. Through the 1980s, the traditional view that medical education enhanced patient care remained intact. So did the long-standing belief that teaching hospitals provided the best patient care—in large part because they were teaching hospitals.

In 1984, the traditional belief that medical education leads to better patient care received a sharp rebuke after 18-year-old Libby Zion died at the New York Hospital. Ms. Zion, a college freshman, had presented to the hospital with several days of a fever and an earache. The next morning she was dead. The case quickly became the center of intense media interest and a cause célèbre for limiting house officer work hours.

The public's fear about the safety of hospitals increased in the 1990s. In 1995, a seeming epidemic of errors, including wrong-site surgery and medication mistakes, erupted at US hospitals. These high-profile tragedies received an enormous amount of media attention. The most highly publicized incident involved the death of 39-year-old Betsy Lehman, a health columnist at the *Boston Globe*, from a massive chemotherapy overdose while being treated for breast cancer at the renowned Dana-Farber Cancer Institute. Public concern for patient safety reached a crescendo in 1999, following the release of the Institute of Medicine's highly publicized report *To Err Is Human*. The report concluded that 48,000 to 98,000 Americans died in US hospitals every year because of preventable medical errors.

The result was that in the early 2000s, a contentious debate concerning resident work hours erupted. Many within the medical profession felt that work-hour regulations need not be imposed. They correctly pointed out that little evidence existed that patients had actually suffered at the hands of overly tired residents, and they also claimed that resident education would suffer if held hostage to a time clock. Critics, particularly from outside the profession, pointed to valid physiological evidence that fatigue causes deterioration of high-level functioning; they also argued that high-quality education cannot occur when residents are too tired to absorb the lessons being taught. As the debate proceeded, the public's voice could not be ignored, for the voices of consumer groups and unions were strong, and Congress threatened legislative action if the profession did not respond on its own

Ultimately, the medical profession acquiesced. In 2002,the Accreditation Council for Graduate Medical Education (ACGME), which oversees and regulates residency programs, established new work-hour standards for residency programs in all specialties. Effective 1 July 2003, residents were not to be scheduled for more than 80 hours of duty per week, averaged over a four-week period. Over-night call was limited to no more frequently than every third night, and residents were required to have one day off per week. House officers were permitted to remain in the hospital for no more than six hours after a night on-call to complete patient care, and a required ten-hour rest period between duty periods was established.

Ironically, as the ACGME passed its new rules, there was little evidence that resident fatigue posed a danger to patients. The Libby Zion case, which fueled the public's concern about resident work hours, was widely misunderstood. The problems in Ms. Zion's care resulted from inadequate supervision, not house officer fatigue. At the time the ACGME established its new rules, the pioneering safety expert David Gaba wrote, "Despite many anecdotes about errors that were attributed to fatigue, no study has proved that fatigue on the part of health care personnel causes errs that harm patients."

On the other hand, the controversy over work hours illustrated a fundamental feature of America's evolving health care system: societal forces were more powerful than professional wishes. The bureaucracy in medical education responded slowly to the public's concerns that the long work hours of residents would endanger patient safety. Accordingly, the initiative for reform shifted to forces outside of medicine—consumers, the federal government, labor, and unions. It became clear that a profession that ignored the public's demand for transparency and accountability did so at its own risk.

KENNETH M. LUDMERER is Professor of Medicine and the Mabel Dorn Reeder Distinguished Professor of the History of Medicine at the Washington University School of Medicine. He is the author of *Learning to Heal: The Development of American Medical Education*, *Time to Heal: American Medical Education from the Turn of the Century to the Era of Managed Care*, and

Let Me Heal: The Opportunity to Preserve Excellence in American Medicine.

Originally published on 7 November 2014 at http://blog.oup.com/2014/11/work-hour-regulations-house-officers/

"Eleanor Roosevelt's last days"

BY PHILIP A. MACKOWIAK

"This blog post initially grabbed me because, though I knew how Franklin Roosevelt died (of a stroke, shortly after Yalta in 1945), I could not say the same about Eleanor Roosevelt. I was unaware of the painful, prolonged, and cruel circumstances of her death in 1962, of a bone marrow disease that was aggressively treated past the point of any hope, and contrary to her own wishes to end treatment. Here we have a case study of a famous patient's last days, but also an introduction to changing medical views on end-of-life care. Reading how celebrities and public figures choose to die—or are denied the choice—made me think about what control ordinary people have over their treatment and care in the face of terminal illness, and sent me back to excellent recent discourse such as Dr. Ken Murray's article in the *Wall Street Journal*, 'Why Doctors Die Differently.'"

—**MAXWELL SINSHEIMER**, Editor, Reference, Oxford University Press

---

When Eleanor Roosevelt died on this day (7 November) in 1962, she was widely regarded as "the greatest woman in the world." Not only was she the longest-tenured First Lady of the United States, but also a teacher, author, journalist, diplomat, and talk-show host. She became a major participant in the intense debates over civil rights, economic justice, multiculturalism, and human rights that remain central to policymaking today. As her husband's most visible surrogate and collaborator, she became the surviving partner who carried their progressive reform agenda deep into the postwar era, helping millions of needy Americans gain a foothold in the middle class, dismantling Jim Crow laws in the South, and transforming the United States from an isolationist into an internationalist power. In spite of her celebrity, or more likely because of it, she had to endure a prolonged period of intense suffering and humiliation before dying, due in large part to her end-of-life care.

Roosevelt's terminal agonies began in April 1960 when at 75 years of age, she consulted her personal physician, David Gurewitsch, for increasing fatigue. On detecting mild anemia and an abnormal bone marrow, he diagnosed "aplastic anemia" and warned Roosevelt that transfusions could bring temporary relief, but that sooner or later, her marrow would break down completely and internal hemorrhaging would result. Roosevelt responded simply that she was "too busy to be sick."

For a variety of arcane reasons, Roosevelt's hematological disorder would be given a different name today—myelodysplastic disorder—and most likely treated with a bone marrow transplant. Unfortunately, in 1962, there was no effective treatment for Roosevelt's hematologic disorder, and over the ensuing two years, Gurewitsch's grim prognosis proved correct. Though she entered Columbia-Presbyterian Hospital in New York City repeatedly for tests and treatments, her "aplastic anemia" progressively worsened. Premarin produced vaginal bleeding, necessitating dilatation and curettage; transfusions provided temporary relief of her fatigue, but at the expense of severe bouts of chills and fever. Repeated courses of prednisone produced only the complications of a weakened immune system. By September 1962, deathly pale, covered with bruises and passing tarry stools, Roosevelt begged Gurewitsch—in vain—to let her die. She began spitting out pills or hiding them under her tongue, refused further tests, and demanded to go home. Eight days after leaving the hospital, the tuberculosis bacillus was cultured from her bone marrow.

Gurewitsch was elated. The new finding, he proclaimed, had increased Roosevelt's chances of survival "by 5000%." Roosevelt's family, however, was unimpressed and insisted that their mother's suffering had gone on long enough. Undeterred, Gurewitsch doubled the dose of tuberculosis medications, gave additional transfusions, ordered tracheal suctioning, and inserted a urinary catheter.

In spite of these measures, Roosevelt's condition continued to deteriorate. Late in the afternoon of 7 November 1962 she ceased breathing. Attempts at closed-chest resuscitation with mouth-to-mouth breathing and intracardiac adrenalin were unsuccessful.

Years later, when reflecting upon these events, Gurewitsch opined that "he had not done well by [Roosevelt] toward the end. She had told him that if her illness flared up again and fatally that she did not want to linger on and expected him to save her from the protracted, helpless, dragging out of suffering. But he could not do it." He said, "When the time came, his duty as a doctor prevented him."

The ethical standards of morally optimal care for the dying we hold dear today had not yet been articulated when Roosevelt became ill and died. Most of them were violated (albeit unknowingly) by Roosevelt's physicians in their desperate efforts to halt the progression of her hematological disorder: that of non-maleficence (i.e., avoiding harm); by pushing prednisone after it was having no apparent therapeutic effect; that of beneficence (i.e., limiting interventions to those that are beneficial); by performing cardiopulmonary resuscitation in the absence of any reasonable prospect of a favorable outcome; that of futility (avoiding futile interventions); and by continuing transfusions, performing tracheal suctioning, and (some might even argue) beginning anti-tuberculosis therapy after it was clear that Roosevelt's condition was terminal.

Roosevelt's physicians also unknowingly violated the principle of respect for persons by ignoring her repeated pleas to discontinue treatment. However, physician-patient relationships were more paternalistic then, and in 1962 many, if not most, physicians likely would have done as Gurewitsch did, believing as he did that their "duty as doctors" compelled them to preserve life at all cost.

Current bioethical concepts and attitudes would dictate a different, presumably more humane, end-of-life care for Eleanor Roosevelt from that received under the direction of Dr. David Gurewitsch. While arguments can be made about whether any ethical principles are timeless, Gurewitsch's own retrospective angst over his treatment of Roosevelt, coupled with ancient precedents proscribing futile and/or maleficent interventions, and an already-growing awareness of the importance of respect for patients' wishes in the early part of the twentieth century, suggest that even by 1962 standards, Roosevelt's end-of-life care was misguided. Nevertheless, in criticizing Gurewitsch for his failure "to save [Roosevelt] from the protracted, helpless, dragging out of suffering," one has to wonder if and when a present-day personal physician of a patient as prominent as Roosevelt would have the fortitude to inform her that nothing more can be done to halt the progression of the disorder that is slowly carrying her to her grave. One wonders further if and when that same personal physician would have the fortitude to inform a deeply concerned public that no further treatment will be given, because in his professional opinion, his famous patient's condition is terminal and further interventions will only prolong her suffering.

Evidence that recent changes in the bioethics of dying have had an impact on the end-of-life care of famous patients is mixed. Former President Richard Nixon and another famous former First Lady, Jacqueline Kennedy Onassis, both had living wills and died peacefully after forgoing potentially life-prolonging interventions. The deaths of Nelson Mandela and Ariel Sharon were different. Though 95 years of age and clearly overmastered by a severe lung infection as early as June 2013, Mandela was maintained on life support in a vegetative state for another six months before finally dying in December of that year. Sharon's dying was even more protracted, thanks to the aggressive end-of-life care provided by Israeli physicians. After a massive hemorrhagic stroke destroyed his cognitive abilities in 2006, a series of surgeries and ongoing medical care kept Sharon alive until renal failure finally ended his suffering in January 2014.

Thus, although bioethical concepts and attitudes regarding end-of-life care have undergone radical changes since 1962, these contrasting cases suggest that those caring for world leaders at the end of their lives today are sometimes as incapable as Roosevelt's physicians were a half century ago in saving their patients from the protracted suffering and indignities of a lingering death.

PHILIP A. MACKOWIAK is Professor and Vice Chairman, Department of Medicine, University of Maryland School of

Medicine, Baltimore, Maryland. He is the author of *Diagnosing Giants: Solving the Medical Mysteries of Thirteen Patients Who Changed the World*.

Originally published on 7 November 2014 at http://blog.oup.com/2014/11/eleanor-roosevelt-end-of-life-care-ethics/

"Jawaharlal Nehru, moral intellectual"

BY MUSHIRUL HASAN

> "Mushirul Hasan's article reflects a crucial moment for Indian scholarship. As India transforms, how does the legacy of our greatest intellectuals inform our future? And the new, global scale of our academic publishing, including scholarly blogs such as this, allows us to have this debate more openly within South Asia and beyond."
>
> —**SUGATA GHOSH,** Director, Global Academic Publishing, India, Oxford University Press

---

In his famous essay, French philosopher Julien Benda indicted intellectuals for treason to their destiny, and blamed them for betraying the very moral principles that made their existence possible. Nehru was not one of them. His avowedly cultural and intellectual orientation is sufficiently well known. His father had refused to perform a purification ceremony on his return from England and had been ostracised by the Brahman orthodoxy. Nehru too didn't submit to irrational authority, be it religion or dogma, though he went along with certain social customs. He did not approve of his father's *shraddha* ceremony, but took part in it for his mother's sake.

Religion and atheism, remarked his niece Nayantara Sahgal, lived lovingly together in Anand Bhawan, and both were aspects of India's enquiring and assimilative mind. The daily life of the Nehrus was a seamless blend of tradition and modernity. This is best exemplified by Nehru's mother and wife Kamala. Both were religious, and yet they lived with Motilal's intellectual modernism and Nehru's scepticism on matters of religion and faith. But in the end their influences prevailed.

Nehru once said to a distinguished author-journalist that the spirit of India was in the depths of his conscience while the mind of the West was in his head (by virtue of what he studied in Harrow, Cambridge, and all over London). He was, thus, driven or dominated by the urge to see reason in people's thinking and action. Sometimes he'd convince them to narrow their differences by concentrating on the "economic factor," but the upsurge of religiosity or the assertion of communitarian identities weakened or nullified his efforts.

Nehru's distance from the masses is too readily assumed. The fact is that he spent years not in comfortable and argumentative exile, but in India itself, where he led the life of an activist with its attendant challenges and hazards. There is a tale, perhaps apocryphal, yet poignant, to the effect that, upon being released from prison after long confinement for speeches he had made, Nehru went directly to a large meeting, stood up and stated quite unaffectedly, "As I was saying . . ."

Nehru placed jail-going as a "trivial matter" in a world that was being shaken to its foundation. His first confinement was in the Lucknow district jail from 6 December 1921 to 3 March 1922; the second from 11 May 1922 to 31 January 1923. In 1930, it was 180 days; in 1931, 99 days; in 1932-33, 612 days; and in 1934-35, 569 days. By March 1938, he had actually spent five-and-a-half years in prison. On 13 March 1945, he had completed over 31 months in Ahmadnagar Fort. From there, he was "repatriated" to Bareilly Central Prison after nearly 32 months. He complained of the typical jail atmosphere—the slow, stagnant, and rather oppressive air, the high walls closing in on him, iron bars and gates, and the noise of the warden at night as he kept watch or counted the prisoners in the different barracks.

All these years, Nehru was moved from one jail to another— to Naini, Lucknow, Bareilly, and Dehradun. Was it worthwhile? In the last paragraph of the *Autobiography*, he explained: "There is no hesitation about the answer. If I were given the chance to go through my life again, with my present knowledge and experience added, I would no doubt try to make many changes in my personal life."

To begin with, the young Nehru had no idea what happened behind the grim gates that swallowed any convict. But soon enough he managed to overcome the nervous excitement and bear an existence full of abnormality, a dull suffering, and a dreadful monotony. His inspiration came from Gandhiji. He had for company his father, who was tried as a member of an "illegal" organisation of Congress volunteers.

One of his fellow inmates commented later that it was ironic that, from an early age, people had started looking upon him as a *desh bhakt*, and he sacrificed his youth and its charms to satisfy public expectations. With arrest and prosecution becoming a frequent occurrence, jails turned into places of pilgrimage. Sometimes he felt as if he richly deserved a spell of jail to make quiet his excitable nature. Sometimes he felt almost cut off from the outside and longed for a quick return. More often than not, he'd wait for a tomorrow to bring deliverance to his people. To his sister Vijaya Lakshmi Pandit he wrote: "Without that steel frame of the mind and body, or spirit if you will, we bend before every wind that blows and disintegrates."

This said, Nehru bore the petty tyrannies of life. With about 50 persons in the barrack, their beds were just about three or four feet apart. The lack of privacy was difficult to endure. "It was the dull side of family life magnified a hundredfold with few of its graces and compensations and all this among people of all kinds and tastes," Nehru aptly remarked. Nights in prison were dreadful, more so with a prisoner snoring, "a gigantic disharmony of ugly noisesgrunt, groan, growl, howl, whine, whistle, hiss, etc. etc."

All day he sat or lay under the *neem* trees, spinning, reading, or writing. At night he'd sit under the starry canopy. Thus, when one of his comrades was promoted to Class A, Nehru felt relieved: "Man is a social animal and too much solitude is not good." But he felt lonely after another friend from his Cambridge days moved to Gonda Jail. His passion was to spin, so he asked for a new *charkha* from Sabarmati Ashram. To write in Urdu, he asked his father to send him an Urdu dictionary. He read newspapers and wrote letters, though he preferred not to read about the battles of his comrades when forced to be idle himself.

Given his sense of movements and changes in history, Nehru agreed that one must follow them without losing sight of the main trend, and that some day, as if by the stroke of a magician's wand, India and the world may be transformed.

MUSHIRUL HASAN is former Professor of History, Jamia Millia Islamia, New Delhi. His previous positions include Director General, National Archives of India, New Delhi (2010–13), and Vice Chancellor, Jamia Millia Islamia, New Delhi (2004–09). He has edited *Nehru's India: Select Speeches* and recently provided a new and comprehensive introduction to *Jawaharlal*

Nehru: A Biography by Sarvepalli Gopal, the authoritative and first-hand account of Nehru. He was awarded the Padma Shri in 2007.

Originally published on 13 November 2014 at http://blog.oup.com/2014/11/jawaharlal-nehru-moral-intellectual/

"Vampires and life decisions"

BY L.A. PAUL

"Academic philosophy has sometimes been criticized for becoming detached from 'the real world.' I think this is unfair: the abstract and the general are just as much part of our world as the concrete and the particular. But in recent years philosophers have increasingly focused on topics which everyone thinks about, to do with the human condition—such as emotion, happiness, the self, and the meaning of life. Laurie Paul has come up with an original approach to a practical problem which we all face: how to make big decisions about our lives, decisions that will themselves transform who we are, making us different people from the people who did the deciding. Her blog post 'Vampires and Life Decisions' is a vivid expression of this key idea."

—**PETER MOMTCHILOFF,** Commissioning Editor, Philosophy, Oxford University Press

---

Imagine that you have a one-time-only chance to become a vampire. With one swift, painless bite, you'll be permanently transformed into an elegant and fabulous creature of the night. As a member of the Undead, your life will be completely different. You'll experience a range of intense new sense experiences; you'll gain immortal strength, speed, and power; and you'll look fantastic in everything you wear. You'll also need to drink the blood of humanely farmed animals (but not human blood), avoid sunlight, and sleep in a coffin.

Now, suppose that all of your friends, people whose interests, views, and lives were similar to yours, have already decided to become vampires. And all of them tell you that they love it. They encourage you to become a vampire too, saying things like: "I'd never go back, even if I could. Life has meaning and a sense of purpose now that it never had when I was human. It's amazing! But I can't really explain it to you, a mere human. You'll have to become a vampire to know what it's like."

In this situation, how could you possibly make an informed choice about what to do? For, after all, you cannot know what it is like to become a vampire until you become one. The experience of becoming a vampire is *transformative*. What I mean by this is that it is an experience that is both radically epistemically new, such that you have to have it in order to know what it will be like for you, and, moreover, will change your core personal preferences.

So you can't rationally choose to become a vampire, but nor can you rationally choose to not become one, if you want to choose based on what you think it would be like to live your life as a vampire. This is because you can't possibly know what it would be like before you try it. And you can't possibly know what you'd be missing if you didn't.

We don't normally have to consider the choice to become Undead, but the structure of this example generalizes, and this makes trouble for a widely assumed story about how we should make momentous, life-changing choices for ourselves. The story is based on the assumption that, in modern Western society, the ideal rational agent is supposed to take charge of her own destiny, mapping out the subjective future she hopes to realize by rationally evaluating her options from her authentic, personal point of view. In other words, when we approach major life decisions, we are supposed to introspect on our past experiences and our current desires about what we want our futures to be like in order to guide us in determining our future selves. But if a big life choice is transformative, you can't know what your future will be like, at least, not in the deeply relevant way that you want to know about it, until you've actually undergone the life experience.

Transformative experience cases are special kinds of cases where important ordinary approaches that people try to use to make better decisions, such as making better generalizations based on past experiences, or educating themselves to better evaluate and recognize their true desires or preferences, simply don't apply. So transformative experience cases are not just cases involving our uncertainty about certain sorts of future experiences. They are special kinds of cases that focus on a distinctive kind of "unknowability"—certain important and distinctive values of the lived experiences in our possible futures are fundamentally first-personally unknowable. The problems with knowing what it will be like to undergo life experiences that will transform you can challenge the very coherence of the ordinary way to approach major decisions.

Moreover, the problem with these kinds of choices isn't just with the unknowability of your future. Transformative experience cases also raise a distinctive kind of decision-theoretic problem for these decisions made for our future selves. Recall the vampire case I started with. The problem here is that, before you change, you are supposed to perform a simulation of how you'd respond to the experience in order to decide whether to change. But the trouble is, who you are changes as you become a vampire.

Think about it: before you become a vampire, you should assess the decision as a human. But you can't imaginatively put yourself in the shoes of the vampire you will become and imaginatively assess what that future lived experience will be. And, after you have become a vampire, you've changed, such that your assessment of your decision now is different from the assessment you made as a human. So the question is, which assessment is the better one? Which view should determine who you become? The view you have when you are human? Or the one you have when you are a vampire?

The questions I've been raising here focus on the fictional case of the choice to become a vampire. But many real-life experiences and the decisions they involve have the very same structure, such as the choice to have one's first child. In fact, in many ways, the choice to become a parent is just like the choice to become a vampire! (You won't have to drink any blood, but you will undergo a major transition, and life will never be the same again.)

In many ways, large and small, as we live our lives, we find ourselves confronted with a brute fact about how little we can know about our futures, just when it is most important to us that we do know. If that's right, then for many big life choices, we only learn what we need to know after we've done it, and we change ourselves in the process of doing it. In the end, it may be that the most rational response to this situation is to change the way we frame these big decisions: instead of choosing based on what we think our futures will be like, we should choose based on whether we want to discover who we'll become.

L.A. PAUL is Professor of Philosophy at the University of North Carolina at Chapel Hill and Professorial Fellow at the University of St. Andrews, Scotland. She is the author of *Transformative Experience*. Her website is www.lapaul.org.

Originally published on 23 November 2014 at: http://blog.oup.com/2014/11/vampires-transformative-experience/

"Rip it up and start again"

BY MATTHEW FLINDERS

> "This was a piece written in a burst of New Year energy. I wanted to make a provocative argument and to say something that I thought really mattered and where there were still opportunities for change. As soon as the piece went live there was an instant online explosion of support for what I was saying. Then a senior political correspondent with the BBC penned a strong rebuttal of my argument that only served to throw petrol on the fire of a debate that was already well alight. What next? A phone call from a group of Northern MPs telling me that my piece had inspired them to start a campaign for a 'Parliament of the North.' Private investors, think tanks, a media launch, a national competition . . . the power of the blog."
>
> —**MATTHEW FLINDERS,** OUPblog columnist and author of *Defending Politics*

"London Bridge is falling down, falling down, falling down; London Bridge is falling down, my fair lady." "Oh no it's not!" I hear you all scream with oodles of post-Christmas pantomime cheer, but Parliament is apparently falling down. A number of restoration and renewal studies of the Palace of Westminster have provided the evidence with increasing urgency. The cost of rebuilding the House? A mere two billion pounds! If it was any other building in the world, its owners would be advised to demolish and rebuild.

The Georgian Parliament Building might be a rather odd place to begin this New Year blog about British politics but the visionary architecture behind the stunning new building in Kutaisi offers important insights for those who care about British politics.

Put very simply, the architecture and design of a building say a lot about the values, principles, and priorities of those working within it. The old parliament building in Tblisi was a stone pillared fortress that reflected the politics of the Soviet era, whereas the new parliament is intended to offer a very public statement about a new form of politics. Its style and design may not be to everyone's taste—a 40-meter-high glass dome that looks like a cross between an alien spaceship and a frog's eye—but the use of curved glass maximises transparency and openness. It represents the antithesis of the stone pillared fortress that went before it.

I'm not suggesting that the London Eye is suddenly upstaged by the creation of a new frog-eye dome on the other side of the Thames, but I am arguing in favour of a little creative destruction. Or to make the same point slightly differently, if we are to spend 2 billion pounds in an age of austerity—and probably far more once the whole refurbishment is complete—then surely we need to spend a little time designing for democracy. Designing for democracy is something that imbued the architecture of the new Scottish Parliament and the National Assembly of Wales; it also underpinned the light and space of the Portcullis House addition to the Palace of Westminster.

The importance of Portcullis House is important. The underground corridor that connects the "old" Palace of Westminster with the "new" Portcullis House is far more than a convenient pathway: it is a time warp that takes the tired MP or the thrusting new intern back and forward between the centuries. The light, modern, and spacious atmosphere of Portcullis House creates an environment in which visitors can relax, committees can operate, and politicians can—dare I say—smile. The atmosphere in the Palace of Westminster is quite different. It is dark and dank. It is as if it has been designed to be off-putting and impenetrable. It is "Hogwarts on Thames," which is great if you have been brought up in an elite public school environment but bad if you have not. It has that smell—you know the one I mean—the smell of private privilege, of a very male environment, of money and assumptions of "class." It is not "fit for purpose" and everyone knows it. And yet we are about to spend billions of pounds rebuilding and reinforcing this structure.

There is, however, a deeper dimension to this plea to take designing for democracy seriously: architecture matters. The structure of Parliament, in terms of the seating and the corridors, the lack of visitor amenities, the lack of windows, and the dominance of dark wood, represents the physical manifestation of that "traditional" mode of British politics that is now so publicly derided. The structure delivers the adversarial "yaa boo" politics that now turns so many people off.

The Palace of Westminster should be a museum, not the institutional heart of British politics.

In recent years the Speakers of both Houses of Parliament have made great strides in terms of "opening up" Parliament, but modernisation in any meaningful sense is fundamentally prevented by the listed status of the building. A window of opportunity for radical reform did open up when an incendiary bomb hit the chamber of the House of Commons on 11 May 1941. The issue of designing for democracy was debated by MPs, with many favouring a transition to a horseshoe or semi-circular design. But in the end, and with the strong encouragement of Winston Churchill, a decision was taken to rebuild the chamber as it had been before in order to reinforce the traditional two-party system. "We shape our buildings," Churchill argued, "and afterwards our buildings shape us." Maybe this is the problem.

The refurbishment of Parliament has so far escaped major public debate and engagement. And yet if we really want to breathe new life into British democracy, then the dilapidation of the Palace of Westminster offers huge opportunities. The 2015 General Election is therefore something of a distraction from the more basic issue of how we design for democracy in the twenty-first century. Fewer MPs but with more resources? Less shouting and more listening? A chamber that can actually seat all of its members? Why not base Parliament outside London and in one of the new "Northern powerhouses" (Sheffield, Manchester, Newcastle) that politicians seem suddenly so keen on? Two billion pounds is a major investment in the social and political infrastructure of the country, so let's be very un-British in our approach, let's design for democracy. Let's do it! Let's rip it up and start again!

MATTHEW FLINDERS is Founding Director of the Sir Bernard Crick Centre for the Public Understanding of Politics at the University of Sheffield and also Visiting Distinguished Professor in Governance and Public Policy at Murdoch University, Western Australia. He is also Chair of the Political Studies Association of the United Kingdom and the author of *Defending Politics*. He loves Parliament but despairs of parliamentary politics and its modus operandi.

Originally published on 7 January 2015 at http://blog.oup.com/2015/01/rebuilding-british-parliament/

"Oppress Muslims in the West. Extremists are counting on it."

BY JUSTIN GEST

"The beauty of the OUPblog is its versatility. Some posts act like a flare: they burn bright for a brief spell, achieving their purpose by illuminating the landscape, but not lingering long. Others remain relevant for years after their debut, such as the numerous postings on paradoxes. To demonstrate the depth and breadth of OUP's publishing, however, a post should meet a number of criteria. It should have a strong argument. It should stand up long after its initial posting. It should be clear, crisp, and compelling. It should be based on empirical research. And it should ideally shed light on an important issue of the day by enlisting the tools and perspectives of the academy to educate those who may not have access to long-form scholarship. Justin Gest's piece on the self-defeating perils of Islamophobia checks all those boxes, and more."

—**NIKO PFUND,** President of OUP USA and Academic Publisher, Oxford University Press

---

In the aftermath of the Paris terror attacks, the Islamophobia pervading Western democracies is the best recruitment tool for violent extremists.

Reports abound about anti-Islam protests, assaults of Muslim civilians, and movements to impose greater surveillance on Western Muslim communities, which have already been disproportionately subjected to "national security" measures.

These are precisely the experiences that provide talking points for extremist groups that might otherwise be frustrated.

I interviewed a number of such Islamic extremists during full-immersion fieldwork in the Bangladeshi community of London's East End and the Moroccan community of Southern Madrid. As part of this research, I also attended over a dozen Islamic extremists' meetings.

In the East End, extremists from the transnational Islamist group Hizb-Ut-Tahrir competed directly against street gangs, schools, sport teams, and mosques for the attention of young Muslim men and women.

For a several weeks, I attended Hizb-Ut-Tahrir gatherings, which took place directly upstairs from a government-sponsored youth club, where neighborhood adolescents went to do homework, play video games, or shoot billiards. Each Thursday after school at about 5:00 pm, a Hizb-Ut-Tahrir activist went into the club downstairs to recruit attendees for their meeting upstairs. They dangled free snacks and soda, and about half of the young men would oblige.

Meetings were run like talk shows. A member would introduce a guest speaker and they would discuss issues pertaining to Islam and British public affairs. Questions came from planted members in the audience, and the young men would listen while chewing and checking their phones.

If it weren't for grievances against the British state and society, these meetings would be more like Quranic study with halal fried chicken.

Instead, there was always much to discuss. In the last decade, the British government extended pre-charge detention periods for terrorism suspects, police imposed greater surveillance on

Muslim groups, and various Islamophobic groups such as the English Defence League and the English National Alliance attacked mosques and Muslim citizens.

For overseas extremists, Europe and North America appear as a fortress. Advanced intelligence and passport control limit the migration of known extremists. And Western Muslims are largely integrated, law-abiding, content members of society. So it is difficult to find recruits or embed them.

Survey research shows that French Muslims are predominantly secular and far less religious than they are portrayed. A recent poll shows that British Muslims identify more closely as British than most non-Muslim Britons. American Muslims, in particular South Asians and Arabs, are among the United States' most affluent, well-educated minorities. And every year, new generations of immigrant-origin Muslims become more integrated into their societies in the West—adapting, intermarrying, having children and grandchildren.

Extremist organizations appeal to the fringes of these communities and must seek out ways to advance their agenda and recruit supporters among the few inclined to listen to their ideology.

Terrorists attacks help, but not by triumphantly assaulting innocent people. Rather terrorism produces an anti-Muslim backlash that frustrates and alienates Muslims over time.

And this backlash creates a sense of betrayal and disappointment among second- and third- generation Western Muslims who believe they are not receiving the equal treatment and justice as the rest of their countrymen.

This backlash corners Western Muslims into a greater awareness of their Muslim-ness. They feel obligated to defend their vilified Muslim identity, when it represents but one facet of their personalities. Muslims are soccer stars and violinists, engineers and drama queens, rappers and politicians. But social scrutiny makes them one-dimensional in the public eye.

This backlash is gold for the Hizb-Ut-Tahrir activist who was previously grasping for something new to inspire the young people sitting in front of him, gnawing on halal fried chicken.

Islamophobia is inherently wrong. But if that is not persuasive enough, it is also an enormous strategic mistake in the struggle against Islamic extremism.

JUSTIN GEST is Assistant Professor of Public Policy at George Mason University's School of Policy, Government, and International Affairs. He is the author of *Apart: Alienated and Engaged Muslims in the West*.

Originally published on 21 January 2015 at http://blog.oup.com/2015/01/islamophobia-muslim-oppression/

"Does philosophy matter?"

BY WALTER SINNOTT-ARMSTRONG

"This blog post was refreshing and timely—two things that I'm usually hoping for in things that I choose to read in my spare time. Sinnott-Armstrong calls out a couple important trends in philosophy that, while maybe particularly egregious in this argument-based, oftentimes macho discipline, are certain to plague others as well: the contempt for people who can't keep up with scholarly arguments or even specific 'in' language and the snobbery towards authors who choose to address the wider public in books written for general readers instead of focusing on super-specialized journal articles. As someone who encounters a lot of dense philosophical prose, I hope that readers cherish what Sinnott-Armstrong says here, in practice and in spirit."

—**LUCY RANDALL,** Editor, Philosophy, Oxford University Press

---

Philosophers love to complain about bad reasoning. How can those other people commit such silly fallacies? Don't they see how arbitrary and inconsistent their positions are? Aren't the counter examples obvious? After complaining, philosophers often turn to humor. Can you believe what they said? Ha, ha, ha. Let's make fun of those stupid people.

I also enjoy complaining and joking, but I worry that this widespread tendency among philosophers puts us out of touch with the rest of society, including academics in other fields. It puts us out of touch partly because they cannot touch us: we cannot learn from others if we see them as unworthy of careful attention and charitable interpretation. This tendency also puts us out of touch with society because we cannot touch them: they will not listen to us if we openly show contempt for them.

One sign of this contempt is the refusal of most philosophers even to try to express their views clearly and concisely enough for readers without extraordinary patience and training. Another sign is that many top departments today view colleagues with suspicion when they choose to write accessible books instead of technical journal articles. Philosophers often risk their professional reputations when they appear on television or write for newspapers or magazines. How can they be serious about philosophy if they are willing to water down their views that much? Are they getting soft?

As a result, philosophers talk only to their own kind and not even to all philosophers. Analytic philosophers complain that continental philosophers are unintelligible. Continental philosophers reply that analytic philosophers pick nits. Both charges contain quite a bit of truth. And how can we expect non-philosophers to understand philosophers if philosophers cannot even understand each other?

Of course, there is a place for professional discourse. Other academic fields from physics to neuroscience also contain tons of technical terms. Professional science journals are rarely enjoyable to read. The difference is that these other fields often work hard to communicate their ideas to outsiders in other venues, whereas most leading philosophers make no such effort. As a result, the general public often sees philosophy as an obscure game that is no fun to play. If philosophers do not find some way to communicate the importance of philosophy, we should not be surprised when nobody else understands why philosophy is important.

This misunderstanding is sad, because philosophy deals with important issues that affect real people. Metaphysicians propose views on free will and causation that could change the way law ascribes responsibility for crimes or limits access to pornography on the grounds that it causes violence to women. Political philosophers defend theories with useful lessons for governments. Philosophers of science raise questions about the objectivity of science that could affect public confidence in evolution or climate change. Philosophers of religion and of human nature present arguments that bear on our place in the universe and nature. Philosophers of language help us understand how we can understand each other when we talk. And, of course, ethicists talk about what is morally wrong or right, good or bad, in situations that we all face and care about.

Because of these potential applications, there must be some way for philosophers to show why and how philosophy is important and to do so clearly and concisely enough that non-philosophers can come to appreciate the value of philosophy. There also must be some way to write philosophy in a lively and engaging fashion, so that the general public will want to read it. A few philosophers already do this. Their examples show that others could do it, but not enough philosophers follow their models. The profession needs to enable and encourage more philosophers to reach beyond the profession.

WALTER SINNOTT-ARMSTRONG is the Philosophy in Action series editor and is the Chauncey Stillman Professor of Practical Ethics in the Department of Philosophy and the Kenan Institute for Ethics at Duke University.

Originally published on 3 March 2015 at http://blog.oup.com/2015/03/does-philosophy-matter/

About the OUPblog

Since 2005, the talented authors, staff, and friends of Oxford University Press provide daily commentary on nearly every subject under the sun, from philosophy to literature to economics. OUPblog is a source like no other on the blogosphere for learning, understanding and reflection, providing academic insights for the thinking world.

The manufacturer's authorised representative in the EU for product safety is Oxford University Press España S.A. of El Parque Empresarial San Fernando de Henares, Avenida de Castilla, 2 – 28830 Madrid (www.oup.es/en or product.safety@oup.com). OUP España S.A. also acts as importer into Spain of products made by the manufacturer.

Printed in the USA/Agawam, MA
July 30, 2026

908341.251